the b

Org

Potat

by

Holly Jones

with

Alan Wilson

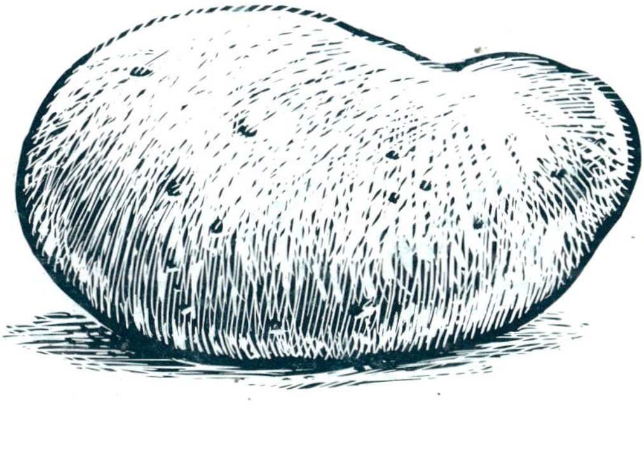

Illustrations by Sarah Williams

for

David

Holly Jones

Holly loves cooking and she loves talking about it; she demonstrates and teaches all over the country and regularly appears on television and radio. Wherever she is, she enthuses people with her passion for cooking with locally produced, seasonal, organic food.

Holly first cooked at Ryton Garden's Potato Day 6 years ago. Inspired by the range of potatoes available, the passion of the contributors and the enthusiasm of the visitors, she has become something of an ambassador for the potato and has now put together this collection of more than 120 recipes.

Holly also works with the National Trust, the BBC and the British Potato Council.

To find out more go to **www.hollychefs.co.uk**

Alan Wilson

Alan Wilson is a self-confessed potato enthusiast who takes his work home with him – as agronomist for the supermarket Waitrose he is involved with potato varieties both professionally and in his own garden.

The Story of the Potato, his first book published in 1993, highlighted the plight of old potato varieties being compromised by the requirements of the National List. In 1994, Alan and HDRA launched the successful Potato Day at Ryton Gardens.

Alan has worked for Waitrose all his working career and is known for his straight talking. His passion and enthusiasm for the huge range of potato varieties is apparent to anyone who has seen him speak at Potato Day.

Acknowledgments

Huge thanks must go to Alan Wilson for his generosity and expertise; Alan and Jackie Gear for their support from my earliest cookery demonstrations at Ryton Gardens; Sarah Williams for her enthusiasm and drawings; Alan Peedle for his vision and design; all friends and family who have been enthusiastic, and at times unwitting, recipe testers and tasters; and David for his encouragement, ideas and endless patience.

www.hollychefs.co.uk

First published in 2001 by Holly Jones.

ISBN 0 9540631 0 4

Additional information by Alan Wilson

Illustrations by Sarah Williams

Designed by Alan Peedle - Acstede Design, www.acstede.com

Printed and bound in England by The Pentagon Press Limited

Contents

Potatoes are the unsung heroes of the vegetable world, but they should be highly valued, if only because of the pleasure they give the nation as chips, let alone as that great comfort food, mashed potato, or my own particular favourite, Pommes Dauphinoise, when they're sliced and baked in the oven with cream and garlic. And there are hundreds of other ways of enjoying them! Of course, organic potatoes, whatever the variety, I think, have a 'superior flavour' because they are grown organically.

Indeed, there are hundreds of individual varieties of potato, each with its own distinctive shape, colour and flavour. Textures, too, make certain types of potato perfect for particular dishes; for example, floury potatoes are good baked, whilst waxy ones are excellent as potato salads.

Genetic diversity is a basic tenet of organic gardening. HDRA, the organic organisation, glories in the richness of the UK's vegetable treasures and has set up the Heritage Seed Library to save as many of these old and threatened vegetables as it can. Hardly surprising then that we also grow many different varieties of potato in our gardens open to the public, and use them to create wonderful, freshly prepared dishes in our restaurants.

Holly Jones shares our love of potatoes. Ever since I launched the first National Potato Day at Ryton Organic Gardens, she has been coming to the event to inspire our visitors with fabulous potato cookery demonstrations. This book has, I am sure, been borne partly out of her association with this wonderful potato celebratory event!

Holly is a brilliant cook and I therefore recommend all these tasty recipes. I have sampled many of them myself and I'm a happier, though heavier woman as a result!

Jackie Gear - Executive Director, HDRA

1

Introduction

Potatoes are such an everyday staple and integral part of British cookery that they are often overlooked in favour of the seemingly more exotic pasta and rice. When they were introduced to Europe from Central America in the 1500's, I can't imagine the Spanish explorers who brought them ever envisaged what an influence they would have.

Since I've been doing the cookery demonstrations at Ryton Gardens' phenomenally successful Potato Day every February, I have been overwhelmed by people's enthusiasm. They come from far and wide to buy their seed potatoes and then grab their seats in the lecture hall for the day's talks.

Every year there are more than 100 varieties of seed potatoes to choose from and the next year, stories of successful, or not so successful, crops abound. This huge selection of potatoes makes me wonder why anyone can categorise them as red or white. The different flavours and textures of each variety can change a dish every time you make it.

There is nothing better than eating freshly-dug new potatoes with butter and mint but there are so many more ways of cooking them. I've put together these potato recipes - some old favourites, some new - and I hope they will give you inspiration and ideas.

The joy of cooking organically for me is working with ingredients through the seasons - using fresh herbs, freshly picked vegetables and full-favoured meat – as well as the knowledge that no chemicals have been used to grow them. Supermarkets have an ever-increasing range of organics but go that step further and seek out your local organic farm shop or stall at the farmers' market to see and buy what is at its peak.

As well as ways of cooking them, this book includes advice on how to grow your potatoes organically, ways of coping with pests, diseases and problems and notes on the huge variety of seed potato available. Alan Wilson has written this, for which I am eternally grateful. Alan is one of the greatest potato heads I know, with patient answers for my endless questions; his excitement and enthusiasm for the potato are infectious.

I hope you enjoy the book and more importantly, continue to enjoy growing, cooking and eating your organic potatoes. As Alan says, the reason we celebrate the potato is its variety and individuality.

Holly Jones

1

- Using Organic Ingredients

- Nutrition

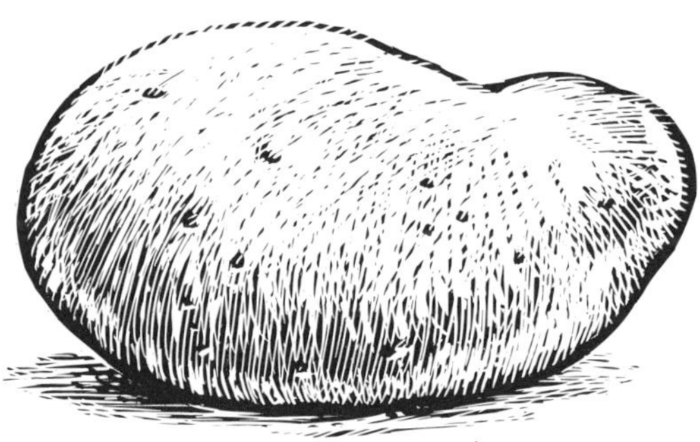

Using Organic Ingredients

Only a couple of years ago, it could be difficult to get hold of organic ingredients. Now it is very easy indeed – there is everything from fruit and veg to baby food, tinned beans, soups, chocolate, ice-cream, beer and wines, oils and vinegars, spices and herbs and the range is growing seemingly daily.

The Organic Directory, published by the Soil Association and Green Books, tells you county by county where you can shop organically. It is easy to buy from the supermarkets who have an increasing range of products but I find independent shops have everything you need and stock good quality, local products such as meats, cheeses, eggs, preserves and breads as well as fruit and vegetables.

One of my favourite organic shops is the Organic Farm Shop near Cirencester, winner of the Soil Association's and You magazine's award for best organic retailer of the year in 2000. Seasonal vegetables and herbs are picked daily from the garden as well as an increasing range of fruit. They sell eggs from their own chickens and meat from their pigs, beef cattle and lambs. Their milk goes to Yeo Valley and returns to the shop in the form of butter and yoghurt. There is a comprehensive range of other groceries and the staff are knowledgeable, enthusiastic and helpful.

For me, this is what organic shopping and cooking is all about – seeing what is available and then planning your meal with fresh seasonal local produce.

I try to keep the following in my store cupboard so I know I can start cooking whenever I need to:–

Oils - Sunflower and olive oil for cooking; extra virgin olive oil for dressings and drizzling over soups and bread.

Vinegars - Red wine, white wine, cider, balsamic and sherry vinegars.

Tins - Tomatoes, baked beans, coconut milk.

Jars - Black and green olives, jams and preserves tahini, grain mustards.

Pulses - Chickpeas, haricot beans, red lentils, Puy lentils, butterbeans.

Spices - Ground cumin, ground coriander, ground ginger, whole nutmeg, whole and ground cinnamon, paprika, cayenne pepper, black peppercorns, turmeric, vanilla pods.

Always buy your spices in small quantities and keep them in the cool and dark.

Herbs - I prefer cooking with fresh herbs but I do use dried bayleaves.

Staples - Brown and white Basmati rice, Arborio rice, wild rice. Different types of pasta. Plain, self-raising and strong flour. Couscous, bulgar wheat and dried noodles. Porridge oats.

Dried Goods - Apricots, prunes, sultanas, raisins. Mushrooms, sun-dried tomatoes.

Nuts and Seeds - Pine kernels, flaked and ground almonds, walnuts, sunflower seeds, sesame seeds.

Sauces and Flavourings - Soy sauce, tamari, chilli sauce, Maldon sea salt.

Nutrition

The potato is packed full of carbohydrates, fibre and vitamin C. It also contains some protein and potassium. All of these are important for a healthy, balanced diet.

Most of the nutrients and fibre are in the skin. I like to cook potatoes with the skin on most of the time – this way, you get all the goodness as it's so easy to throw it away with the peelings. Remember to scrub the tubers well to get rid of any dirt. Leaving the skin on also helps to keep the flesh together, especially those varieties that can collapse on cooking.

The most vitamin C is in those potatoes that have just been lifted. Stored potatoes contain less. The best way to keep vitamin C in cooking is to bake or fry the potatoes. Boiled and mashed potatoes have the least as it leaches out in the cooking water.

Carbohydrates are vital for energy and the potato is full of them. Nineteenth century Irish farm labourers would eat an astounding 8-10lb of potatoes every day.

We used to think potatoes were fattening but this is due to the toppings used – butter, cheese, cream, crème fraiche. Cooked without fat – i.e., baked or boiled, the potato is very satisfying and low in fat.

Green potatoes contain poisons, even small amounts of which can cause headaches and drowsiness in susceptible people. Throw them away and check your stored potatoes regularly for signs of greening or rotting.

- Cooking the Recipes in this Book

I'm very much of the opinion that recipes should be a guideline. If you want to try one but don't have exactly what's written, then adapt them for your kitchen and family and also what's in season.

All the recipes feed **6** so if you're cooking for smaller numbers, just halve the ingredients or make the whole dish and put the rest in the freezer.

I haven't specified what kind of potato to use in which recipe besides floury or waxy – this very much depends on what you have grown or bought and each variety will give different results.

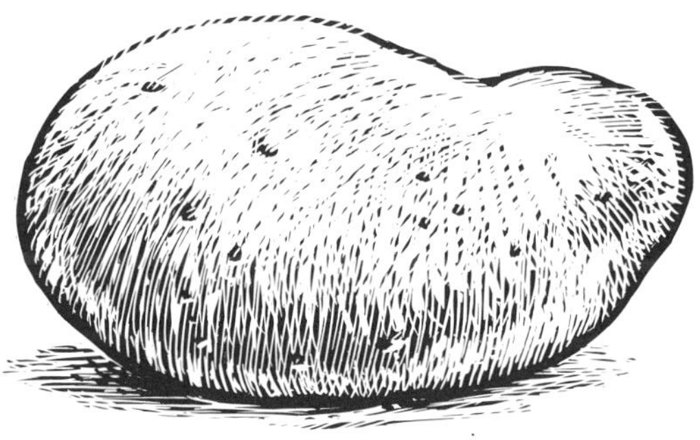

notes

3

Potato
- Soups
- Salads

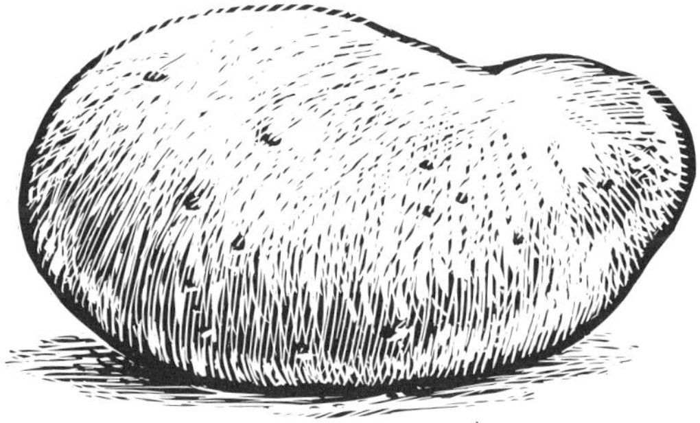

Vegetable Stock

It's very quick and easy to make your own vegetable stock and I think it has a better flavour than packet stock.

2	Onions, peeled and roughly chopped
2	Carrots, peeled and roughly chopped
2	Sticks celery, roughly chopped
1	Tomato, chopped
1	Broccoli stalk, roughly chopped
1	Bayleaf
6	Peppercorns
2	Sprigs parsley
2	Sprigs thyme

1. Put everything in a large saucepan and cover with water.
2. Bring to the boil and simmer gently for 15-20 minutes.
3. Strain and cool. Use as required.

Chicken Stock

1	Cooked chicken carcass including skin
2	Carrots, peeled and roughly chopped
1	Onion, peeled and quartered
1	Leek, trimmed, well-washed and chopped
2	Stalks celery, roughly chopped
6	Black peppercorns
2	Dried bayleaves
4	Fresh parsley stalks
2	Sprigs fresh thyme

1. Put everything into a large pan and cover with water.
2. Bring to the boil and skim off any scum that has formed.
3. Cover and simmer very gently for 2-3 hours.
4. Strain into a large bowl and allow to cool. Refrigerate overnight.
5. Skim off any fat that has formed on the surface.

Use within 3 days or freeze. To freeze, reduce the stock by half by boiling vigorously and cool. Pour into ice-cube trays and freeze. When frozen put the cubes into a bag, label it, and when you want to use one, just put in a jug and add boiling water to dissolve the cube.

Pea, Potato and Mint Soup

15ml / 1 tbsp	Sunflower oil
2	Onions, peeled and chopped
500g / 1lb 2oz	Floury potatoes, peeled and chopped
$1\frac{1}{2}$ litres / $2\frac{1}{2}$ pints	Water
500g / 1lb 2oz	Peas
60g / 2oz	Fresh mint, chopped
	Salt and pepper

1. Heat the oil and sweat the onions and potatoes over a gentle heat for 5 minutes.
2. Season well and add the water. Bring to the boil and simmer until the potatoes are tender. Add the peas and simmer for another 5 minutes.
3. Take off the heat and add the mint. Whizz with a hand blender until smooth.

Chicken and Potato Soup

280g / 10oz	Cooked chicken, skinned and shredded
500g / 1lb 2oz	Potatoes, peeled and cubed
225g / 8oz	Leeks, trimmed, washed and sliced
2 tbsp	Fresh chopped parsley
1 tsp	Paprika
1½ litres / 2½ pints	Chicken stock
15ml / 1 tbsp	Sunflower oil
	Salt and pepper

1. Heat the oil in a large pan and add the leeks, potatoes and paprika. Cook for 3-4 minutes and cover with the chicken stock. Season well and bring to the boil. Simmer until the potatoes are tender.
2. Take off the heat and whizz with a hand blender until the vegetables have thickened the stock but some chunks still remain.
3. Stir in the chicken pieces and heat through. Stir in the parsley and serve.

Potato, Sweet Potato and Spinach Soup

500g / 1lb 2oz	Potatoes, peeled and cubed
500g / 1lb 2oz	Orange sweet potatoes, peeled and cubed
2	Leeks, trimmed, sliced and well washed
2	Cloves garlic, peeled and crushed
250g / 8oz	Spinach, washed and de-stalked
15ml / 1 tbsp	Sunflower oil
1½ litres / 2½ pints	Vegetable stock
	Salt and pepper

1. Heat the oil in a large pan and add the potatoes, sweet potatoes, leeks and garlic. Cook for 2 minutes and cover with the stock. Season with salt and pepper.
2. Bring to the boil and simmer for 15 minutes until the potatoes are tender.
3. Take off the heat and whizz the soup until smooth with a hand blender.
4. Shred the spinach and stir into the soup. Allow to wilt in the heat for 2 minutes and then serve.

Leek and Potato Soup

This is a classic potato soup. If served chilled, it is known as Vichyssoise. Traditionally, only the whites of the leeks would be used but I prefer to use the green as well as it gives more flavour and colour. Do remember to wash the leeks really well first so that you get rid of any grit in the layers.

500g / 1lb 2oz	Potatoes, peeled and cubed
500g / 1lb 2oz	Leeks, trimmed, sliced and washed
1	Onion, peeled and sliced
1 litres / 1¾ pints	Vegetable stock
3 tbsp	Chopped fresh parsley
60 ml / 2 fl oz	Double cream
15ml / 1 tbsp	Sunflower oil
	Salt and pepper

1. Heat the oil in a large pan and add the potatoes, onion and leeks.
2. Add the stock and season well. Cover, bring to the boil and simmer for 15-20 minutes until the potatoes are tender.
3. Take off the heat and whizz until smooth with a hand blender. Stir in the cream and chopped parsley and serve.

Leek and Potato Soup with Coconut Milk

500g / 1lb 2oz	Potatoes, peeled and cubed
500g / 1lb 2oz	Leeks, trimmed, sliced and washed
1 x 400ml / 14 fl oz	Tin coconut milk
600ml / 1 pint	Vegetable stock
3 tbsp	Chopped fresh coriander
1	Fresh red chilli, deveined, deseeded and finely chopped
15ml / 1 tbsp	Sunflower oil
	Salt and pepper

1. Heat the oil in a large pan and add the potatoes, leeks and chilli.
2. Add the stock and coconut milk and season well. Bring to the boil and simmer for 15-20 minutes until the potatoes are tender.
3. Take off the heat and whizz until smooth with a hand blender. Stir in the chopped coriander and serve.

Spiced Potato Soup

1kg / 2¼ lb	Potatoes, peeled and cubed
2	Onions, peeled and sliced
2	Cloves garlic, peeled and crushed
1 tsp	Ground coriander
1 tsp	Ground cumin
2 tsp	Paprika
	Juice and zest 1 lemon
3 tbsp	Fresh coriander, chopped
1½ litres / 2½ pints	Vegetable stock
15ml / 1 tbsp	Sunflower oil
	Salt and pepper

1. Heat the oil in a large pan and add the onions and the potatoes. Cook for 2 minutes. Stir in the garlic, spices, lemon juice and zest and cook for another minute.
2. Add the stock and season well. Bring to the boil and simmer for 15 minutes until the potatoes are tender.
3. Take off the heat and whizz until smooth with a hand blender. Stir in the chopped coriander and serve.

Chunky Bean Soup with Potatoes

1 x 400g / 14 oz	Tin chopped tomatoes
1 x 400g / 14 oz	Tin mixed pulses, drained
450g / 1lb	Potatoes, washed and diced
2	Red onions, peeled and thinly sliced
2	Cloves garlic, peeled and crushed
2 tbsp	Parsley, finely chopped
1 tsp	Paprika
15ml / 1 tbsp	Sunflower oil
	Salt and pepper

1. Heat the oil in a large saucepan and stir in the onions, garlic and potatoes. Cook for 2 minutes. Stir in the paprika and half the parsley and cook for another minute.
2. Add the tomatoes and 400ml / 14 fl oz water, season well and bring to the boil. Simmer for 10-15 minutes until the potatoes are tender. Whizz until still slightly chunky with a hand blender.
3. Stir in the beans and heat through. Stir in the rest of the parsley and serve.

Potato and Haddock Chowder with Chives

1 kg / 2¼ lb	Undyed smoked haddock
700g / 1½ lb	Waxy potatoes, washed and cubed
2	Leeks, trimmed, sliced and washed
1 tsp	Paprika
15ml / 1 tbsp	Sunflower oil
1½ litres / 2½ pints	Milk
30g / 1oz	Crème fraiche
2 tbsp	Freshly chopped chives
	Salt and pepper

1. Put half the milk in a large pan and bring to a gentle simmer. Add the bayleaf and fish, skin side up. Cook very gently until the fish is just starting to flake.
2. Turn off the heat and take the fish out. Drain the milk and reserve. Skin and bone the fish and flake into large chunks.
3. Put the oil in a large pan and add the leeks, paprika and potatoes. Cook for 2 minutes and add all the milk. Add pepper and salt if it is needed – remember the fish may be salty.
4. Bring to the boil and simmer gently for 15-20 minutes until the potatoes are tender. Whizz until still slightly chunky with a hand blender.
5. Add the haddock flakes and heat through. Stir in the chives and crème fraiche and serve.

Butterbean Soup with Potatoes and Chilli

2 x 400g / 14 oz	Tins butterbeans, drained
500g / 1lb 2oz	Waxy potatoes, washed and cubed
1	Leek, trimmed, sliced and washed
1	Red chilli, deseeded, deveined and finely chopped
2	Cloves garlic, peeled and crushed
1 tbsp	Fresh thyme leaves
2 tbsp	Chopped fresh parsley
1½ litres / 2½ pints	Vegetable stock
15ml / 1 tbsp	Sunflower oil
	Salt and pepper

1. Heat the oil and add the potatoes, leek, chilli and garlic. Cook for 2 minutes and stir in the thyme and the stock. Season well.
2. Bring to the boil, cover and simmer for 15 minutes until the potatoes are tender.
3. Add the butterbeans and parsley and heat through. Whizz until still slightly chunky with a hand blender and serve.

Potato and Herb Soup

This soup changes its character throughout the year as you can use different herbs in season.

700g / 1½ lb	Potatoes, peeled and cubed
2	Onions, peeled and sliced
1½ litres / 2½ pints	Vegetable stock
15ml / 1 tbsp	Sunflower oil
60g / 2oz	Sorrel, shredded
2 tbsp	Freshly chopped parsley
1 tbsp	Freshly chopped chives
1 tbsp	Freshly chopped marjoram
	Salt and pepper

1. Heat the oil in a large pan and add the onions and the potatoes. Cook for 2 minutes, season well and add the stock.
2. Bring to the boil and simmer until the potatoes are tender. Off the heat, add the herbs and allow the sorrel to wilt.
3. Whizz until smooth with a hand blender and serve.

Spinach and Potato Soup

If you make this with spinach that has just come out of the garden, the taste is amazing – sweet and earthy. Use the same quantities to make watercress soup.

500g / 1lb 2oz	Potatoes, peeled and cubed
2	Leeks, trimmed, washed and sliced
340g / 12oz	Fresh spinach, well washed, destalked and shredded
1½ litres / 2½ pints	Vegetable stock
15ml / 1 tbsp	Sunflower oil
	Salt and pepper

1. Heat the oil in a large pan and add the potatoes and the onions. Season well and add the stock. Cover, bring to the boil and simmer until tender.
2. Add the spinach and cook for 5 minutes. Whizz until smooth with a hand blender and serve.

Potato, Swede and Nettle Soup

Nettle tops are good to make soup when they are young. Remember to pick them with gloves on from a quiet spot in the garden and wash them well.

450g / 1lb	Potatoes, washed and cubed
280g / 10oz	Swede, peeled and cubed
200g / 7oz	Young nettle tops
2	Onions, peeled and sliced
2	Cloves garlic, peeled and crushed
1 tbsp	Thyme leaves
1½ litres / 2½ pints	Vegetables stock
15ml / 1 tbsp	Sunflower oil
	Salt and pepper

1. Heat the oil in a large pan and add the potatoes, swede, onions and garlic. Season well and add the stock and thyme. Cover, bring to the boil and simmer until tender.
2. Add the nettle tops and cook for 5 minutes. Whizz until smooth with a hand blender and serve.

Roast Corn and Potato Chowder

4	Corn cobs
500g / 1lb 2oz	Potatoes, washed and cubed
1	Green pepper, deseeded, deveined & diced
1	Green chilli, deseeded, deveined and finely chopped
1	Clove garlic, peeled and crushed
1½ litres / 2½ pints	Vegetable stock
15ml / 1 tbsp	Sunflower oil
	Salt and pepper

1. Heat the oven to 200°C / 400°F / Gas 6. Put the corn on a baking sheet and bake for 30 minutes until starting to turn golden brown. Cool and take the kernels off the cob. (You can also do this on a barbecue)
2. Heat the oil in a large pan and add the onions, potatoes, chilli, green pepper, garlic and corn. Cook for 2 minutes and season well.
3. Add the stock and bring to the boil. Cover and simmer until the potatoes are tender but not falling apart.
4. Whizz with a hand blender until the soup is still half chunky.

Potato and Kale Soup with Miso

You can make this soup with curly kale, red Russian kale or Italian cavolo nero. If you can't get kale, Swiss chard or Savoy cabbage work well.

700g / 1½ lb	Potatoes, washed and cubed
500g / 1lb 2oz	Kale, washed and finely shredded
1½ litres / 2½ pints	Vegetable stock
2	Cloves garlic, peeled and crushed
2 tbsp	Miso dissolved in 2 tbsp boiling water
15ml / 1 tbsp	Sunflower oil
	Salt and pepper

1. Heat the oil and add the potatoes, garlic and stock. Season well. Bring to the boil and simmer until the potatoes are tender but not collapsing.
2. Stir in the miso and kale and cook gently until the kale is tender. Serve.

Tomato, Potato and Black Pudding Soup

This is soup is really delicious and satisfying. It also works well with other continental-style sausages like chorizo.

2 x 400g / 14 oz	Tins chopped tomatoes
2	Onions, peeled and sliced
2	Cloves garlic, peeled and crushed
120ml / 4 fl oz	Red wine
1 tsp	Sugar
1	Bayleaf
1	Sprig thyme
1 tsp	Paprika
15ml / 1 tbsp	Sunflower oil
450g / 1lb	Waxy potatoes, washed and cubed
200g / 7oz	Black pudding, skinned and cubed
600ml / 1 pint	Chicken stock
2 tbsp	Freshly chopped parsley
	Salt and pepper

1. Heat the oil and add the onions and garlic and cook for 2 minutes. Add the bayleaf, thyme, paprika, sugar, wine and tomatoes and season well. Bring to the boil and simmer for 20 minutes.
2. Discard the thyme and bayleaf and whizz until smooth with a hand blender.
3. Add the potatoes and the stock and bring to the boil. Simmer gently until the potatoes are tender.
4. Stir in the black pudding and parsley and heat through. Serve.

Potato and Chestnut Soup

500g / 1lb 2oz	Potatoes, peeled and cubed
500g / 1lb 2oz	Fresh chestnuts, cooked and peeled
120ml / 4 fl oz	Dry white wine
2 tbsp	Sage leaves, finely chopped
2	Red onions, peeled and finely diced
1	Clove garlic, peeled and crushed
1½ litres / 2½ pints	Vegetable stock
15ml / 1 tbsp	Sunflower oil
4	Spring onions, shredded
	Salt and pepper

1. Heat the oil and add the red onions and garlic.
2. Add the chestnuts to the pan with the potatoes, sage and stock and season well.
3. Bring to the boil and simmer gently until the potatoes are tender.
4. Whizz until still half chunky with a hand blender. Stir in the spring onions and serve.

You can also use dried chestnuts in this recipe. Soak 225g / 8oz dried chestnuts in water overnight and drain.

Spicy Potato and Cauliflower Soup

450g / 1lb	Potatoes, diced
450g / 1lb	Cauliflower florets
1	Onion, peeled and sliced
15ml / 1 tbsp	Sunflower oil
1 tsp	Ground cumin
1 tsp	Ground coriander
½ tsp	Ground turmeric
½ tsp	Chilli powder
1	Clove garlic, peeled and crushed
	Juice of 1 lemon
1½ litres / 2½ pints	Vegetable stock
2 tbsp	Chopped fresh coriander
	Salt and pepper

1. Heat the oil and add the onion, potatoes and cauliflower. Stir for 3-4 minutes and add the garlic and all the spices. Cook for another minute, season well and stir in the stock.
2. Bring to the boil and cover. Simmer gently for 15-20 minutes until the cauliflower and potatoes are tender.
3. Stir in the lemon juice and whizz until smooth with a hand blender. Stir in the coriander and serve.

Creamy Potato Soup with Thyme and Bacon

1 kg / 2¼ lb	Floury potatoes, peeled and cubed
2	Onions, peeled and sliced
2	Cloves garlic, peeled and crushed
120ml / 4 fl oz	Dry white wine
200g / 7oz	Smoked streaky bacon, derinded & chopped
2 tbsp	Fresh chopped thyme
1½ litres / 2½ pints	Chicken stock
120g / 4oz	Crème fraiche
15ml / 1 tbsp	Sunflower oil
	Salt and pepper

1. Dry fry the bacon in a non-stick frying pan until crisp and drain on kitchen paper.
2. Heat the oil in a saucepan and add the onions, potatoes and garlic. Cook for 2 minutes and add the wine. Bubble to reduce by half. Add half the thyme, season well and add the chicken stock. Bring to the boil and simmer until the potatoes are tender.
3. Add the crème fraiche and whizz until smooth with a hand blender. Stir in the cooked bacon and the rest of the thyme and heat through. Serve.

Winter Vegetable Soup

280g / 10oz	Each of potatoes, carrots, swede and celeriac, peeled, washed and cubed
150g / 5oz	Parsnips, peeled and cubed
2	Onions, peeled and sliced
2	Cloves garlic, peeled and crushed
1½ litres / 2½ pints	Vegetable stock
1	Bayleaf
2	Sprigs parsley
1	Sprig fresh thyme
15ml / 1 tbsp	Sunflower oil
	Salt and pepper

1. Heat the oil in a large saucepan and add all the vegetables. Season well and add the bayleaf, parsley, thyme and stock.
2. Bring to the boil, cover and simmer until all the vegetables are completely tender.
3. Remove the herbs and whizz until smooth with a hand blender.

Summer Vegetable Soup

500g / 1lb 2oz	Salad potatoes, thinly sliced
1	Bunch spring onions, trimmed & shredded
1	Red pepper, deseeded, deveined and cubed
200g / 7oz	French beans, trimmed and chopped
120g / 4oz	Broad beans
120g / 4oz	Peas
2	Courgettes, trimmed and cubed
200g / 7oz	Spinach, destalked, washed and shredded
2 tbsp	Chopped fresh mint
2 tbsp	Chopped fresh marjoram
1 tbsp	Shredded sorrel leaves
1½ litres / 2½ pints	Vegetable stock
120ml / 4 fl oz	Dry white wine
15ml / 1 tbsp	Olive oil
	Salt and pepper

1. Heat the oil and add the potatoes, spring onions and red pepper. Add the white wine and stock and season well. Cover and simmer very gently until the potatoes are almost tender.
2. Stir in the peas, courgettes, French beans and broad beans. Bring to the boil and simmer for 5 minutes until the vegetables are all tender.
3. Turn the heat off and stir in the spinach – allow to wilt for 2-3 minutes.
4. Stir in the mint, marjoram and sorrel and serve.

Bean and Potato Soup with Basil

500g / 1lb 2oz	Waxy potatoes, washed and cubed
500g / 1lb 2oz	Mixed beans (French beans, runner beans, broad beans, peas)
2	Red onions, peeled and finely sliced
1	Clove garlic, peeled and crushed
1½ litres / 2½ pints	Vegetable stock
30g / 1oz	Crème fraiche
2 tbsp	Shredded fresh basil
1 tbsp	Chopped fresh parsley
15ml / 1 tbsp	Olive oil
	Salt and pepper

1. Heat the oil and add the onions, garlic and potatoes. Cook gently for 5 minutes until starting to soften and add the stock.
2. Season well, bring to the boil and simmer for 10 minutes until the potatoes are almost cooked.
3. Add the bean mixture and simmer for another 5 minutes until they and the potatoes are tender.
4. Stir in the herbs and crème fraiche, heat through and serve hot or at room temperature.

Roast Beetroot and Potato Salad

500g / 1lb 2oz	Raw beetroot, washed and trimmed
500g / 1lb 2oz	Waxy potatoes, washed
150ml / 5 fl oz	Natural yoghurt
30g / 1oz	Sunflower seeds, toasted
1 tbsp	Chopped fresh parsley
15ml / 1 tbsp	Mayonnaise
15ml / 1 tbsp	Cider vinegar

1. Heat the oven to 200°C / 400°F / Gas 6.
2. Put the beetroot in a roasting tin and roast until tender – up to 1 hour. Cool and then skin. Cut into dice.
3. Cook the potatoes in boiling water until tender. Drain, cool and dice.
4. Mix together the yoghurt, mayonnaise, cider vinegar and parsley and season well. Mix in the beetroot, potatoes and sunflower seeds.

Potato Salad with Red Pepper Dressing

1 kg / 2¼ lb	Small waxy potatoes, well washed
2	Red peppers
2 tbsp	Finely chopped parsley
1	Bunch spring onions, trimmed and finely shredded
150ml / 5 fl oz	Plain yoghurt
15ml / 1 tbsp	Red wine vinegar
	Salt and pepper

1. Heat the oven to 200°C / 400°F / Gas 6.
2. Put the peppers in a roasting tin and bake for 30 minutes until they wrinkle and deflate. Allow to cool until you can handle them and take off the skin and the stalk. Remove the seeds but try to keep the juice.
3. Using a hand blender, whizz together the pepper flesh and juice with the yoghurt, vinegar and parsley and season well.
4. Boil the potatoes until tender, halve if necessary and toss with the red pepper dressing whilst still hot. Stir in the shredded spring onions and serve hot or at room temperature.

Hot Potato and Bacon Salad

1 kg / 2¼ lb	Waxy potatoes, washed and sliced
1	Red onion, peeled and sliced
2	Cloves garlic, peeled and crushed
120g / 4oz	Streaked smoky bacon, derinded & chopped
15ml / 1 tbsp	Olive oil
15ml / 1 tbsp	Red wine vinegar
2 tbsp	Mixed chopped fresh herbs
	Salt and pepper

1. Boil the potatoes in their skins until tender.
2. Heat the oil and cook the onion, garlic and bacon.
3. Drain the potatoes, toss with the bacon mixture and gently stir in the vinegar and the herbs.
4. Season with pepper and salt if necessary and serve at once.

Potato Salad with Black Olives, Cherry Tomatoes and Herb Dressing

1 kg / 2¼ lb	Small waxy potatoes, washed and halved
120g / 4oz	Black olives, pitted and roughly chopped
120g / 4oz	Cherry tomatoes, cut in half
2	Cloves garlic, peeled and crushed
1 tbsp	Each fresh thyme, parsley and chives
90ml / 3 fl oz	Olive oil
30ml / 2 tbsp	Cider vinegar
	Salt and pepper

1. Cook the potatoes in salted boiling water until tender and drain.
2. Whizz together the oil, vinegar, herbs and garlic with a hand blender and add a little salt and pepper.
3. Add the dressing to the potatoes while they are still hot and toss thoroughly.
4. Gently stir in the olives and tomatoes. Serve hot or at room temperature.

Potato Salad with Fennel, Green Beans and Smoked Mackerel

1 kg / 2¼ lb	Small waxy potatoes, washed and halved
2	Bulbs fennel, trimmed and very finely sliced
200g / 7oz	French beans, trimmed
1	Fillet smoked mackerel, skinned and flaked
45ml / 3 tbsp	Sunflower oil
	Juice and zest 1 lemon
1 tsp	Grain mustard
3 tbsp	Chopped fresh chives

1. Boil the potatoes until tender and drain. Lightly steam the French beans and cool.
2. Whizz together the oil, lemon juice and zest and mustard with a hand blender and pour over the hot potatoes, tossing to combine.
3. When the potatoes have cooled, gently stir in the flaked mackerel, fennel, chives and French beans. Serve at room temperature.

Chicken and Potato Salad with Green Goddess Dressing

This delicious dressing was invented at the Palace Hotel in San Francisco in 1915. It also goes well with salmon, lobster and prawns.

500g / 1lb 2oz	Small new potatoes, washed and quartered
500g / 1lb 2oz	Cold roast chicken, skinned and shredded
120ml / 4 fl oz	Sour cream
60ml / 2 fl oz	Mayonnaise
	Juice and zest 1 lemon
2	Anchovies, mashed
1 tbsp	Chopped fresh tarragon
1	Clove garlic, peeled and crushed
2 tbsp	Chopped fresh parsley
4	Spring onions, trimmed and finely shredded
	Salt and pepper

1. Boil the potatoes until tender and drain.
2. Mix together the sour cream, mayonnaise, lemon juice and zest, tarragon, parsley, garlic and anchovies. Season to taste.
3. Toss the potatoes in the dressing and gently stir in the chicken and spring onions.

Broad Bean, Potato and Feta Salad with Mint Dressing

500g / 1lb 2oz	Broad beans, shelled weight
500g / 1lb 2oz	Salad potatoes, washed and sliced
200g / 7oz	Feta cheese, diced
2 tbsp	Each chopped fresh mint and marjoram
15ml / 1 tbsp	White wine vinegar
45ml / 3 tbsp	Olive oil
1	Clove garlic, peeled and crushed
	Salt and pepper

1. Steam the potatoes and the beans separately until tender.
2. Whizz together the herbs, vinegar, garlic and oil with a hand blender and season.
3. Pour over the hot beans and potatoes and when cool, fold in the Feta.

Potato, Leek, Pear and Blue Cheese Salad

500g / 1lb 2oz	Pink fir apples, washed and cut in half lengthways
500g / 1lb 2oz	Leeks, trimmed and well washed
1	Ripe pear, cored and finely diced
120g / 4oz	Roquefort or other blue cheese, crumbled
45ml / 3 tbsp	Sunflower oil
15ml / 1 tbsp	Red wine vinegar
2 tbsp	Chopped fresh tarragon
	Ground black pepper

1. Steam the potatoes and leeks separately until tender.
2. Mix together the oil, vinegar and tarragon with plenty of ground black pepper and toss with the potatoes, leeks and pears.
3. Gently fold in the Roquefort and serve at room temperature.

Roast Potato Salad with Beans and Tomato Dressing

1 kg / 2¼ lb	Salad potatoes, washed and quartered
500g / 1lb 2oz	French beans, trimmed
240g / 8oz	Ripe tomatoes, chopped
30ml / 2 tbsp	Red wine vinegar
90ml / 6 tbsp	Olive oil
1	Clove garlic, peeled and crushed
	Handful fresh basil
	Salt and pepper

1. Heat the oven to 220°C / 425°F / Gas 7.
2. Toss the potatoes in 2 tbsp of the oil and put in a roasting tin. Bake for 45 minutes until golden and tender.
3. Add the beans and roast for another 10-12 minutes until starting to char.
4. Using a hand blender, whizz the tomatoes with the vinegar, garlic, basil and the rest of the oil until smooth.
5. Put the potatoes and beans in a large bowl and toss with the tomato dressing. Serve at once.

Potato Salad with Satay Dressing

1 kg / 2¼ lb	Salad potatoes, scrubbed and quartered
1	Bunch spring onions
1	Red pepper, deseeded, deveined and finely diced
85g / 3oz	Peanut butter
2	Red chillies, deseeded and deveined
2	Cloves garlic, peeled and crushed
60ml / 4 tbsp	Red wine vinegar
60ml / 4 tbsp	Tamari or soy sauce
90ml / 3 fl oz	Water

1. Boil the potatoes until tender; drain and cool. Mix with the red pepper and spring onions.
2. Using a hand blender, whizz the peanut butter, chillies, garlic, vinegar, tamari and water to get a smooth dressing.
3. Pour over the potatoes and serve.

Garlic Potato Salad

1 kg / 2¼ lb	Salad potatoes, scrubbed and halved
6	Cloves garlic, peeled and crushed
90ml / 3 fl oz	Olive oil
30ml / 1 fl oz	White wine vinegar
1 tsp	Sugar
2	Red onions, peeled and finely sliced
2 tbsp	Chopped fresh chives
	Salt and pepper

1. Boil the potatoes until tender and drain.
2. Whizz together the oil, vinegar, sugar and garlic with a hand blender and season.
3. Stir in the onions and chives and pour over the potatoes whilst still hot.

Greek Potato Salad

700g / 1½ lb	Salad potatoes, washed and sliced
120g / 4oz	Green olives, pitted and roughly chopped
3 tbsp	Fresh chopped coriander or marjoram
60ml / 4 tbsp	Red wine vinegar
120g / 4oz	Feta Cheese, cubed
2	Green peppers, deseeded, deveined and cubed
1	Red chilli, deseeded, deveined and finely chopped
	Salt and pepper

1. Boil the potatoes until tender and drain. Mix with the olives and vinegar while still hot and cool to room temperature.
2. Gently fold in the rest of the ingredients and serve at room temperature.

Potato and Citrus Salad with Yoghurt and Coriander

700g / 1½ lb	Waxy potatoes, washed and quartered
1	Pink grapefruit
2	Oranges
150ml / 5 fl oz	Plain yoghurt
15ml / 1 tbsp	White wine vinegar
3 tbsp	Chopped fresh coriander
60g / 2oz	Sunflower seeds, toasted
	Salt and pepper

1. Boil the potatoes until tender and drain.
2. Peel the grapefruit and oranges making sure you get rid of all the pith. Take out any seeds and chop roughly. Save any juice that comes out.
3. Mix the yoghurt with the fruit juice, vinegar and coriander and season. When the potatoes are cool, mix with the fruit, yoghurt dressing and sunflower seeds and serve at room temperature.

Mixed Bean and Potato Salad with Basil and Rocket

Serve this salad with some good bread or plainly grilled chicken - fantastic eaten outside during late summer evenings. The lemon basil has a real zing to it but if you can't get it, ordinary basil works too.

340g / 12oz	Waxy potatoes, washed
225g / 8oz	Runner beans, trimmed and sliced
225g / 8oz	French beans, trimmed
180g / 6oz	Sugarsnap peas
4	Handfuls rocket leaves
60g / 2oz	Lemon basil leaves
6 tbsp	Olive oil
2 tbsp	Red wine vinegar
	Salt and pepper

1. Boil the potatoes until tender, cool and slice. Steam the beans and peas until tender and cool.
2. Put the potatoes, beans and peas into a large bowl with the rocket and basil. Add the olive oil and vinegar. Season well and toss thoroughly together.
3. Serve at once.

Potato and Spinach Salad with Pinenuts and Sultanas

1 kg / 2¼ lb	Waxy potatoes, washed and cubed
340g / 12oz	Baby spinach, trimmed, washed and dried
1	Red onion, peeled and finely sliced
60g / 2oz	Pinenuts, toasted
60g / 2oz	Sultanas
2 tbsp	Chopped fresh mint
6 tbsp	Olive oil
2 tbsp	Red wine vinegar
	Salt and pepper

1. Cover the sultanas in boiling water for 4-5 minutes to plump up. Drain and cool.
2. Boil the potatoes until tender, drain and cool.
3. Toss everything together in a large bowl and season well.

Potatoes in Olive Oil and Pepper

The secret of this dish is to make it well in advance so the onions still retain their flavour but lose their crunch and rawness.

1½ kg / 3 lb 6oz	Floury potatoes, peeled and roughly chopped
2	Red onions, peeled and finely sliced
300ml / 10 fl oz	Good olive oil
	Large bunch flat-leaf parsley, chopped
	Plenty of freshly ground black pepper

1. Boil the potato chunks until tender.
2. Drain and mix with the olive oil, onions and plenty of freshly ground black pepper.
3. Leave to marinate for 12 hours.
4. Stir in the parsley and serve at room temperature.

Potato - Main Courses

- *with meat*
- *with fish*
- *vegetarian*

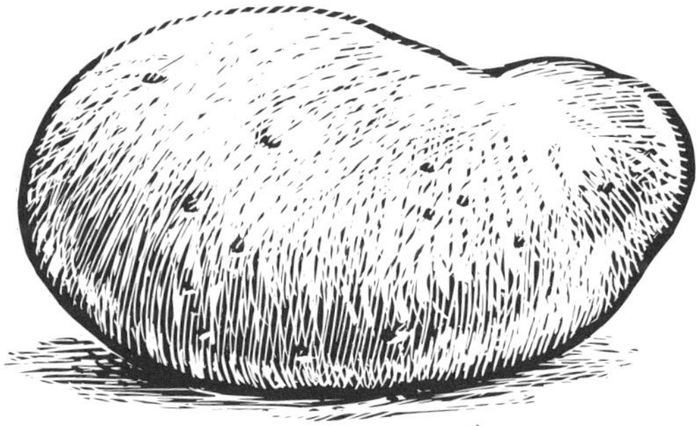

Potato, Bacon and Leek Torte

750g / 1lb 12oz	Waxy potatoes, parboiled, peeled and sliced
4	Leeks, trimmed, washed and sliced
120g / 4oz	Smoked streaky bacon, derinded & chopped
2 tbsp	Chopped fresh chives
2 tbsp	Chopped fresh parsley
1 tbsp	Grain mustard
150ml / 5 fl oz	Dry white wine
60g / 2oz	Crème fraiche
15ml / 1 tbsp	Sunflower oil
30g / 1oz	Butter
	Salt and pepper

1. Heat the oven to 190°C / 375°F / Gas 5. Lightly oil a 20 cm / 8 inch loose-bottomed cake tin.
2. Heat the oil and cook the leeks and bacon until the leeks are soft. Add the wine and bubble to reduce by half. Season well.
3. Off the heat, stir in the mustard, crème fraiche and herbs. Season well.
4. Make a layer of ⅓ of the potatoes in the tin. Cover with half the leek mixture. Repeat. Finish with a final layer of potatoes on top.
5. Dot the butter over the top.
6. Bake in the oven for 30-40 minutes until the cake is golden and piping hot.
7. Serve cut into wedges.

Moroccan-Spiced Lamb with Potatoes and Spinach

1kg / 2¼ lb	Shoulder of lamb, trimmed of fat and cut into 5 cm / 2 inch cubes
600g / 1lb 5 oz	Waxy potatoes, washed and cut into 2½ cm / 1 inch cubes
2 x 400g / 14oz	Tins chopped tomatoes
200g / 7oz	Baby spinach, washed
120g / 4oz	Sultanas
2	Onions, peeled and sliced
2	Cloves garlic, peeled and crushed
1 tbsp	Ground coriander
1 tbsp	Ground cumin
1 tsp	Paprika
1 tbsp	Chopped fresh thyme leaves
30ml / 2 tbsp	Red wine vinegar
300ml / ½ pint	Lamb stock
30ml / 2 tbsp	Sunflower oil
	Salt and pepper

1. Heat the oven to 170°C / 325°F / Gas 3.
2. Heat half the oil in a large ovenproof casserole dish and brown the lamb over a high heat. Keep to one side. Put the rest of the oil in the pan and heat. Add the onions and the garlic and cook for 3 minutes until starting to soften.
3. Stir in the spices and cook for 1 minute. Add the potatoes, sultanas, lamb, thyme, vinegar and tomatoes. Season well and add the lamb stock.
4. Bring to the boil, cover with a lid and put in the oven for 2 hours.
5. When the meat and the potatoes are tender, stir in the spinach and allow to wilt.

Chicken, Vegetable and Potato Pie

Thigh meat works well in this pie as it has lots of flavour. You can make this dish in advance up to the end of stage 4 – cool and reheat until piping hot when you want to eat.

500g / 1lb 2oz	Chicken, skinned, boned and diced
750g / 1lb 11oz	Potatoes, peeled and sliced
2	Carrots, peeled and diced
225g / 8oz	Squash, peeled, seeded and cubed
2	Leeks, washed and sliced
2 tbsp	Chopped fresh parsley
30ml / 2 tbsp	Sunflower oil
60g / 2oz	Plain flour
600ml /1 pint	Chicken stock
30g / 1oz	Butter
	Salt and pepper

1. Heat the oven to 200˚C / 400˚F / Gas 6.
2. Bring a pan of water to the boil and par-boil the potato slices for 3-4 minutes. Drain and cool.
3. Heat the oil in a large pan and add the leeks, carrots and squash. Cook for 4-5 minutes until starting to soften. Add the chicken and cook for 3 more minutes. Stir in the flour, season well and cook for 2 minutes. Stir in the chicken stock and bring to the boil, stirring all the time. Simmer gently for 10 minutes.
4. Stir in the parsley and turn into an ovenproof dish. Arrange the potatoes in a layer over the top. Dot over the butter.
5. Bake in the oven for 30 minutes until the top is golden and the pie is piping hot.

Potato, Pumpkin and Bacon Tortilla

340g / 12oz	Pumpkin or butternut squash, peeled, deseeded and grated
340g / 12oz	Potatoes, peeled and grated
120g / 4oz	Smoked streaky bacon, derinded & chopped
30ml / 2 tbsp	Sunflower oil
1	Red onion, peeled and sliced
1	Red chilli, deseeded and finely chopped
60g / 2oz	Parmesan cheese, grated
6	Eggs, beaten
	Salt and pepper

1. Heat the oil in an ovenproof frying pan. Cook the onion and the bacon until starting to soften. Add the grated pumpkin and potato.
2. Mix the eggs with the cheese and chilli and season well. Stir in the pumpkin mixture and mix together.
3. Pour back into the pan and press down. Bake in a preheated oven – 190˚C / 375˚F / Gas 5 – for 10 minutes until set.
4. Serve warm or at room temperature cut into wedges.

For a vegetarian dish, leave out the bacon.

Potato Hash

This is based on corned beef hash but you can use any meat; you could also use a flavoured mash. This is a great way to use up leftovers so, if you like, add peas, sliced cooked mushrooms or tomatoes as well.

500g / 1lb 2oz	Mashed potatoes
2	Onions, peeled and chopped
500g / 1lb 2oz	Shredded cooked meat – roast beef or lamb both work well
30ml / 2 tbsp	Sunflower oil
15ml / 1 tbsp	Grain mustard
2 tbsp	Chopped fresh parsley
	Salt and pepper

1. Heat the oil and add the onions. Cook for 5 minutes until softened.
2. Mix with the potatoes, meat, mustard and parsley in a large bowl and season well.
3. Heat a non-stick frying pan and pile in the potato mixture. Press down into a round cake and cook over a medium heat until golden and crunchy.
4. Slide on to a plate and flip the uncooked side into the pan to cook until golden brown and crunchy.
5. Serve hot with baked beans.

Panhacketty

8	Large, good quality pork sausages
450ml / 1 pint	Dry cider
15ml / 1 tbsp	Cider vinegar
1	Bramley apple, peeled, cored and diced
1	Cox's apple, peeled, cored and diced
450g / 1lb	Waxy potatoes, peeled and cubed
15ml / 1 tbsp	Olive oil
2	Red onions, peeled and sliced
1	Clove garlic, peeled and crushed
225g / 8oz	Streaky smoked bacon, derinded & chopped
15g / ½ oz	Plain flour
	Few sprigs fresh thyme
2	Bayleaves
	Salt and pepper

1. Heat the oil in a heavy saucepan. Fry the sausages until browned all over and keep on a plate.
2. Add the onions, bacon and garlic and cook for about 5 minutes.
3. Add the flour and season. Stir and cook for 2 minutes. Add the cider and vinegar and bring to the boil, stirring as you do so. Add the thyme, bayleaves, potatoes, apples and sausages. Cover with a tight fitting lid and simmer gently on a low heat for 40 minutes.

Potato, Celeriac and Bacon Gratin

500g / 1lb 2oz	Waxy potatoes, washed, sliced and parboiled
500g / 1lb 2oz	Celeriac, peeled, sliced and parboiled
2	Onions, peeled and sliced
200g / 7oz	Smoked streaky bacon, derinded and chopped
200g / 7oz	Crème fraiche
150ml / 5 fl oz	Dry white wine
2 tbsp	Finely chopped fresh parsley
15ml / 1 tbsp	Sunflower oil
	Salt and pepper

1. Heat the oven to 200°C / 400°F / Gas 6.
2. Heat the oil in a frying pan and add the onions and the bacon. Cook until the onions are soft and golden. Add the wine and bubble to reduce by half. Off the heat, stir in the crème fraiche and parsley and season well.
3. Lightly oil a shallow ovenproof dish. Mix the potatoes, celeriac and onion mixture together and turn into the dish.
4. Bake in the oven for 30 minutes until piping hot and golden brown.

Cottage Pie

500g / 1lb 2oz	Floury potatoes, peeled and cubed
280g / 10oz	Swede, peeled and cubed
900g / 2lb	Minced beef
200g / 7oz	Onions, peeled and finely chopped
200g / 7oz	Carrots, peeled and finely chopped
2	Sticks celery, finely chopped
2	Cloves garlic, peeled and crushed
450ml / ¾ pint	Beef stock
30ml / 2 tbsp	Tomato ketchup
1 tsp	Balsamic vinegar
1 tsp	Ground cumin
15ml / 1 tbsp	Sunflower oil
15g / ½ oz	Plain flour
	Salt and pepper

1. Heat a non-stick frying pan and add the minced beef in batches. Break up with a fork and fry over a high heat to colour the meat. Drain off any fat.
2. In another pan, heat the oil and add the onions, carrots, celery and garlic. Cook gently for 5 minutes until softened. Stir in the cumin and the flour. Cook for 2 minutes and stir in the stock, ketchup and vinegar. Season well. Bring to the boil, stir in the browned mince and simmer for 30 minutes.
3. Boil the potatoes and swede together until tender. Drain, mash and season well.
4. Heat the oven to 200°C / 400°F / Gas 6. Put the mince mixture into an ovenproof dish and top with the mashed potatoes and swede. (At this point you can chill and reheat when needed). Bake for 40 minutes until golden brown and piping hot.

Hotpot

1½ kg / 3lb 6oz	Floury potatoes, washed and thinly sliced
12	Lamb chops
6	Lamb's kidneys, cored and chopped
3	Onions, peeled and thinly sliced
600ml / 1 pint	Lamb stock
30ml / 2 tbsp	Sunflower oil
	Salt and pepper

1. Heat the oven to 180°C / 350°F / Gas 4.
2. Heat the oil and quickly fry the chops and kidneys to colour them.
3. Layer the potatoes, onions, chops and kidneys in an ovenproof casserole dish, seasoning as you do so. Finish with a layer of potatoes.
4. Heat the stock to boiling point and pour into the casserole.
5. Cover and bake in the oven for 2 hours until the potatoes are tender.

Irish Stew

1 kg / 2¼ lb	Floury potatoes, washed and cubed
500g / 1lb 2oz	Boned shoulder of lamb, cubed
3	Onions, peeled and sliced
500g / 1lb 2oz	Carrots, peeled and cubed
1 litre / 1¾ pints	Lamb stock
1	Bay leaf
1 tbsp	Fresh thyme leaves
2 tbsp	Freshly chopped parsley
2 tbsp	Sunflower oil
	Salt and pepper

1. Heat the oven to 170°C / 325°F / Gas 3.
2. Heat the oil and brown the lamb, onions and carrots in batches.
3. Put all the ingredients into a flameproof casserole, season well and cover. Bring to the boil, put in the oven and bake for 3 hours until the vegetables and meat are tender.

Potato, Bacon and Pea Frittata

450g / 1lb	Waxy potatoes, washed and cubed
2	Red onions, peeled and sliced
150g / 5oz	Bacon, derinded and chopped
150g / 5oz	Frozen peas, defrosted
1 tbsp	Chopped fresh tarragon
6	6 eggs
15ml / 1 tbsp	Sunflower oil
85g / 3oz	Parmesan cheese, grated
	Salt and pepper

1. Heat the oven to 190˚C / 375˚F / Gas 5.
2. Steam the potatoes until tender and cool.
3. Heat the oil in an ovenproof frying pan and cook the onions and bacon until the onions have softened. Take off the heat.
4. Add the peas, potatoes and tarragon and season well. Stir together. Beat the eggs and pour over the ingredients in the pan. Sprinkle over the Parmesan cheese and bake in the oven for 10 minutes until the eggs have set.
5. Slide onto a plate, cut into wedges and serve hot or at room temperature with some good bread and a mixed green salad.

Lamb and Potato Patties with Mint and Coriander Sauce

These are delicious with a crispy green salad in hot pitta bread. As well as frying them you can also cook them on the barbecue or roast them in a hot oven – 200°C / 400°F / Gas 6 – for 20 minutes.

500g / 1lb 2oz	Minced lamb
500g / 1lb 2oz	Waxy potatoes
1	Red onion, peeled and very finely chopped
2	Cloves garlic, peeled and finely crushed
1 tsp	Paprika
1 tsp	Ground cumin
2 tbsp	Chopped fresh parsley
1	Beaten egg
	Sunflower oil
	Salt and pepper

1. Boil the potatoes and when tender, drain and cool. Skin and cut into 2mm / ¼ inch dice.
2. Mix the potatoes with the lamb, onion, garlic, spices, egg and parsley and season well.
3. Shape into 12 patties and chill for 1 hour.
4. Heat 2mm / ¼ inch sunflower oil in a large frying pan and cook the patties in batches until browned on each side and cooked through.

Mint and Coriander Sauce

2 tbsp	Each chopped fresh mint and coriander
150ml / 5 fl oz	Natural yoghurt
2 tbsp	White wine vinegar
1 tsp	Caster sugar
	Plenty of freshly ground black pepper

Whizz all the ingredients together with a hand blender and chill until needed.

Apple and Ham Rosti

750g / 1½ lb	Potatoes, peeled and grated
120g / 4oz	Cooked ham, finely shredded
2	Apples, cored and grated
1	Bunch spring onions, peeled and shredded
1 tbsp	Chopped fresh herbs e.g. tarragon, parsley, chives
30g / 1oz	Butter
30ml / 2 tbsp	Olive oil
	Salt and pepper

1. Put the grated potato in a clean towel and squeeze out all the liquid. Mix with the ham, apples, spring onions and herbs and season well.
2. Melt the butter and the oil together in a non-stick frying pan and when foaming, add the potato mixture.
3. Cook gently until golden brown and slide the rosti on to a plate. Add a little more butter and oil to the pan if dry and return the rosti to the pan, cooked side up.
4. When the bottom is golden brown, cut the rosti into wedges and serve with a green salad.

Fisherman's Pie

This is a classic – it does require advance preparation but you can get it ready, get all the clearing up done and then bake it when you want to eat.

2kg / 2¼ lb	Waxy potatoes, washed, parboiled, peeled and sliced
2kg / 2¼ lb	White or smoked fish or a mixture
1 litre / 1¾ pint	Milk
60g / 2oz	Butter
3	Leeks, thinly sliced and well washed
60g / 2oz	Plain flour
120g / 4oz	Frozen peas, defrosted
120g / 4oz	Cooked, peeled prawns
3 tbsp	Chopped fresh parsley
30ml / 2 tbsp	Sunflower oil
	The juice of 1 lemon
	Salt and pepper

1. Put the fish in a large saucepan and cover with the milk. Bring to the boil and simmer for 8-10 minutes until just cooked. Skin, bone and flake the fish and reserve the milk.
2. Heat the oven to 190°C / 375°F / Gas 5.
3. Melt the butter in a saucepan and add the leeks. Cook for 5 minutes until soft. Add the flour and stir in. Cook for 2 minutes. Stir in the reserved milk to make a sauce. Bring to the boil and simmer gently for 10 minutes. Stir in the lemon juice and parsley and season well.
4. Put the fish in an ovenproof dish with the bacon, peas and prawns and cover with the sauce. Slice the potatoes and arrange on the top, overlapping them as you do so.
5. Brush with the oil and bake for 30 minutes until the top is golden brown and crisp and the pie is piping hot.

Soufflé Potato Pancakes with Smoked Salmon and Crème Fraiche

450g / 1lb	Smooth mashed potatoes
6	Eggs, separated
200g / 7oz	Smoked salmon
120g / 4oz	Crème fraiche
2 tbsp	Chopped fresh dill plus 12 sprigs
30ml / 2 tbsp	Sunflower oil
	Salt and pepper

1. Mix the egg yolks and chopped dill into the mashed potato and season well. Whisk the egg whites until they are at the soft peak stage and fold into the potatoes.
2. Heat the oil in a frying pan and add spoonfuls of the mixture. Cook until golden brown on each side and puffed up. You will probably have to do this in batches so keep the cooked pancakes warm while you cook the others. You should end up with 12 pancakes.
3. Put a spoonful of crème fraiche on each pancake and top with a generous piece of smoked salmon and a sprig of dill.

Fish Cakes with Tomato Sauce

450g / 1lb	Mashed potato
450g / 1lb	Cooked fish, boned and skinned (salmon, trout, cod, haddock...)
1	Beaten egg
2 tbsp	Chopped fresh chives and parsley
	Salt and pepper
	Plain flour
	Sunflower oil

1. Gently mix together the fish and potato and season well. Stir in the herbs and bind with the egg. Shape into 12 patties, toss gently in plain flour and chill thoroughly.
2. Heat 2mm / ¼ inch oil in a wide frying pan and shallow fry the patties until crisp and golden on the outside and heated right through. Serve with home-made tomato sauce and green salad

Tomato Sauce

2	Medium onions, peeled and finely chopped
1 x 400g / 14oz	Tin chopped tomatoes
1	Stick celery, finely chopped
1	1 carrot, peeled and finely chopped
1	1 clove garlic, peeled and crushed
15ml / 1 tbsp	Sunflower oil
	Salt and pepper

1. Heat the olive oil in a saucepan and add the onion, celery, carrot and garlic. Cook gently for 5 minutes.
2. Add the tomatoes and season well. Bring to the boil and simmer gently, uncovered, for 20 minutes until thick and jammy. Whizz until smooth with a hand bender.

Grilled Trout with Asparagus, Potatoes and Salsa Verde

This is colourful and delicious. As the asparagus season is so short, you can make this dish with broccoli instead – the purple sprouting variety is fantastic.

6	Trout fillets
900g / 2lb	Waxy potatoes, well washed
450g / 1lb	Asparagus, trimmed
	Large handful fresh parsley
	Large handful fresh basil
	Small handful fresh mint
3	Cloves garlic
30g / 1oz	Capers, drained
3	Anchovy fillets, drained
2 tbsp	Red wine vinegar
6 tbsp	Olive oil
1 tbsp	Mild grain mustard
	Salt and pepper

1. Boil the potatoes until cooked and drain. Steam the asparagus until tender.
2. Heat the grill and cook the trout fillets for 4-5 minutes.
3. **Salsa Verde** - Whizz together the herbs, garlic, capers, anchovies, vinegar, oil and mustard with a hand blender to make the salsa verde. Season to taste.
4. Toss the potatoes and asparagus together with the salsa verde and pile up on 6 plates. Place a grilled trout fillet on top of each pile and serve at once.

Potato, Glazed Onion and Prune Cake

1kg / 2¼ lb	Waxy potatoes, parboiled, peeled and sliced
1kg / 2¼ lb	Onions, peeled and sliced
120g / 4oz	Pitted prunes, chopped
2 tbsp	Chopped fresh chives
2 tbsp	Chopped fresh parsley
15g / 1 tbsp	Grain mustard
30ml / 2 tbsp	Balsamic vinegar
60g / 2oz	Crème fraiche
30g / 1oz	Butter
15ml / 1 tbsp	Sunflower oil
	Salt and pepper

1. Heat the oven to 190°C / 375°F / Gas 5. Lightly oil a 20cm / 8 inch loose-bottomed cake tin.
2. Heat the oil and cook the onions really slowly until caramelised – about 45 minutes. This looks like a lot of onions initially but they will decrease in volume.
3. Off the heat, stir in the mustard, crème fraiche, vinegar, prunes and herbs. Season well.
4. Make a layer of 1/3 of the potatoes in the tin. Cover with half the onion mixture. Repeat. Finish with a final layer of potatoes on top.
5. Dot over the butter.
6. Bake in the oven for 30-40 minutes until the cake is golden and piping hot. Cut into wedges and serve.

Spicy Potato and Chickpea Stew

225g / 8oz	Cooked chickpeas
450g / 1lb	Waxy potatoes, washed and cubed
2	Red onions, peeled and sliced
3	Cloves garlic, peeled and crushed
1 tsp	Ground cumin
1 tsp	Ground coriander
1	Fresh green chilli, deveined, deseeded and finely chopped
2½cm / 1 inch	Piece root ginger, peeled & finely chopped
1 x 400g / 14oz	Tin chopped tomatoes
300ml / ½ pint	Vegetable stock
15ml / 1 tbsp	Sunflower oil
	Juice and zest 1 lemon
2 tbsp	Fresh coriander leaves
	Salt and pepper

1. Heat the oil and gently fry the onions, potatoes and garlic for 2-3 minutes.
2. Stir in all the spices and cook for another 2 minutes.
3. Stir in the tomatoes, stock and chickpeas and season well.
4. Bring to the boil and simmer until the potatoes are tender.
5. Stir in the lemon juice and zest and fresh coriander and serve with rice.

Aubergine and Potato Stew

450g / 1 lb	Potatoes, washed and cut into 1cm cubes
15ml / 1 tbsp	Olive oil
2	2 garlic cloves, peeled and crushed
2	2 onions, peeled and sliced
1 (about 400g / 14oz)	Aubergine, cut into 1 cm / ½ inch cubes
1 x 400g / 14oz	Tin chopped tomatoes
300ml / 10 fl oz	Vegetable stock
15ml / 1 tbsp	Balsamic vinegar
2 tbsp	Chopped fresh parsley
	Large handful fresh basil, shredded
	Salt and pepper

1. Heat the oil and cook the onion, garlic, potatoes and aubergine for 3-4 minutes.
2. Add the tomatoes, stock and balsamic vinegar and bring to the boil. Season. Simmer for about 20 minutes until the potatoes and aubergine are tender.
3. Stir in the parsley and basil and serve.

Spiced Roots with Coconut and Lemon

500g / 1lb 2oz	Waxy potatoes, washed
2	Carrots, peeled
2	Parsnips, peeled
1	Medium celeriac, peeled
1	Swede, peeled
15ml / 1 tbsp	Sunflower oil
1 tsp	Paprika
1 tsp	Ground coriander
2	Cloves garlic, peeled and crushed
1 x 400ml / 14 fl oz	Tin coconut milk
	Juice and zest 3 lemons
4 tbsp	Chopped fresh coriander
	Salt and pepper

1. Cut all the vegetables into batons 5cm / 2 inches long and ½ cm / ¼ inch across.
2. Heat the oil in a large pan and add the vegetables. Stir in the spices and garlic and cook for 2-3 minutes.
3. Stir in the coconut milk, lemon juice and lemon zest. Bring to the boil, cover and simmer gently over a low heat until the vegetables are tender.
4. Stir in the fresh coriander and serve.

Variations – You can make other versions of this by adding chicken or prawns

Latkes

240g / 8oz	Grated raw potato
2	2 eggs, beaten
15g / ½ oz	Plain flour
1	Small onion, peeled and very finely chopped
1 tbsp	Chopped fresh parsley
	Salt and pepper
	Sunflower oil for frying

1. Mix together the potato, eggs, flour, onion and parsley and season well.
2. Heat 2-3 tbsp of the oil in a frying pan, ideally non-stick.
3. Drop tablespoons of the mixture into the hot oil and fry the latkes until golden brown on both sides.
4. Serve at once with sour cream.

Savoury Bread and Butter Pudding with Goat's Cheese and Thyme

½	Loaf potato and herb bread (see chapter on cakes, pastry and bread)
85g / 3oz	Black olives, pitted and chopped
2 tbsp	Fresh thyme leaves
1 tbsp	Chopped fresh chives
6	Eggs
280g / 10oz	Crème fraiche
300ml / ½ pint	Milk
1	Bunch spring onions, trimmed and finely shredded
120g / 4oz	Goat's cheese, crumbled
	Salt and pepper

1. Heat the oven to 180°C / 350°F / Gas 4.
2. Cut the bread into 2½ cm / 1 inch cubes and put into a large shallow dish. Add the herbs, olives, spring onions and goat's cheese and mix together.
3. Beat together the eggs, milk and crème fraiche and season well. Pour over the bread mixture and leave to soak for 20 minutes.
4. Bake in the oven until the pudding is set but still slightly wobbly – about 30 minutes. Serve hot with a salad.

Swiss Chard, Potato and Gruyère Gratin

You can use other greens for this dish – kale, cabbage, leeks, even beetroot tops work well.

1kg / 2¼ lb	Waxy potatoes, washed, parboiled and sliced
500g / 1lb 2oz	Swiss chard
3	Onions, peeled and sliced
2	Cloves garlic, peeled and crushed
15ml / 1 tbsp	Sunflower oil
200g / 7oz	Crème fraiche
150ml / 5 fl oz	Dry white wine
180g / 6oz	Gruyère cheese, grated
2 tbsp	Chopped fresh chives
30g / 1oz	Butter
	Freshly grated nutmeg
	Salt and pepper

1. Heat the oven to 200°C / 400°F / Gas 6. Lightly grease a shallow ovenproof dish.
2. Take the Swiss chard leaves off the stalks. Finely slice the stalks and shred the leaves.
3. Heat the oil and fry the onions and garlic until soft and golden.
4. Add the sliced chard stalks and cook for 3 minutes, stir in the leaves and allow to wilt. Add the wine and bubble to reduce by half. Take off the heat and stir in the crème fraiche, grated cheese, chives, some grated nutmeg and season well.
5. Layer the potatoes and chard mixture ending with a layer of potatoes. Dot the butter over the top and bake in the oven for 30 minutes until golden and bubbling.

Braised Potatoes with Wild Mushrooms

675g / 1½ lb	Waxy potatoes, washed and cubed
200g / 7oz	Chestnut mushrooms, sliced
15g / ½oz	Dried porcini, soaked in 2 tbsp boiling water
2	Red onions, peeled and sliced
2	Cloves garlic, peeled and crushed
600ml / 1 pint	Vegetable stock
1 tbsp	Fresh thyme leaves
2 tbsp	Chopped fresh parsley
15ml / 1 tbsp	Sunflower oil
	Salt and pepper

1. Heat the oil in a large pan and add the onions and garlic. Cook for 2 minutes and then add the potatoes, mushrooms and porcini with their soaking liquor. Add the thyme and stock and season well.
2. Bring to the boil and simmer until the potatoes are tender and the stock has reduced. Stir in the parsley and serve.

Spiced Potatoes with Spinach

This dish is very flexible – you can serve it as a main course with rice or couscous, serve it as a side dish with plain grilled meat or fish, and even serve it cold as a salad. Instead of the spinach, try using other vegetables such as broccoli, cauliflower or squash but add them to the pan with the potatoes.

900g / 2 lb	Potatoes, washed and cubed
2	Onions, peeled and sliced
2	Cloves garlic, peeled and crushed
1	Fresh green chilli, deveined, deseeded and finely chopped
1 tsp	Ground coriander
1 tsp	Ground cumin
1 tsp	Turmeric
½ tsp	Ground ginger
15 ml / 1 tbsp	Sunflower oil
300ml / ½ pint	Water
450g / 1lb	Spinach, washed, destalked and shredded
150g / 5 fl oz	Natural yoghurt
2 tbsp	Chopped fresh coriander
	Salt and pepper

1. Heat the oil and add the onions, garlic and chilli. Cook for 5 minutes. Stir in the spices and cook gently for 2 minutes.
2. Stir in the potatoes, season well and add the water. Bring to the boil, cover tightly and simmer gently until the potatoes are tender.
3. Stir in the spinach and allow to wilt for 2-3 minutes. Off the heat, stir in the yoghurt and fresh coriander and serve.

Potato Cakes with Roast Red Pepper and Olives

600g / 1lb 5oz	Mashed potato
2	Red peppers
85g / 3oz	Black olives, pitted and chopped
2 tbsp	Chopped fresh chives
1	Clove garlic, peeled and crushed
15ml / 1 tbsp	Olive oil
	Salt and pepper

1. Heat the oven to 200°C / 400°F / Gas 6. Put the peppers in a roasting tin and roast for 30 minutes until wrinkly and deflated. Cool, skin and deseed. Whizz to a purée in a food processor.
2. Mix the purée into the mash with the chopped olives, garlic and chives. Season well. Shape into 6 patties and chill.
3. Heat the oil in a frying pan and fry the patties for 3-4 minutes on each side until golden and heated through. Serve with a mixed green salad and watercress sauce.

Watercress Sauce

Whizz together 1 bunch watercress with 150ml / 5 fl oz natural yoghurt, 1 tbsp white wine vinegar, plenty of black pepper and the juice and zest of 1 lemon.

White Bean, Potato and Rosemary Stew

This stew is very satisfying but does take some time to cook so make it in advance and reheat.

450g / 1 lb	Dried cannellini or haricot beans, soaked overnight
4	Cloves garlic, peeled
2	Sprigs fresh sage
675g / 1½ lb	Waxy potatoes, washed and cubed
6	Red onions, peeled and sliced
3 tbsp	Chopped fresh parsley
3 tbsp	Chopped fresh rosemary
1	Fresh red chilli, deveined, deseeded and finely chopped
3 tbsp	Olive oil
	Salt and pepper

1. Drain and rinse the beans and put in a large saucepan with the garlic, 1 tbsp of the oil and the sage. Cover and bring to the boil. Boil hard for 10 minutes and then simmer until tender – 2-3 hours.
2. Heat the rest of the oil and cook the onions very slowly in it until soft and melting. Stir in the herbs and chilli and season well.
3. Boil the potatoes until tender and drain.
4. When the beans are tender, drain but reserve some of the cooking liquor.
5. Mix the beans with the potatoes and onions mixture and heat through. Add a little of the bean liquor if too dry.
6. Serve with a green salad and lots of crusty bread.

Potato - Side Dishes - Cakes, Pastries & Breads

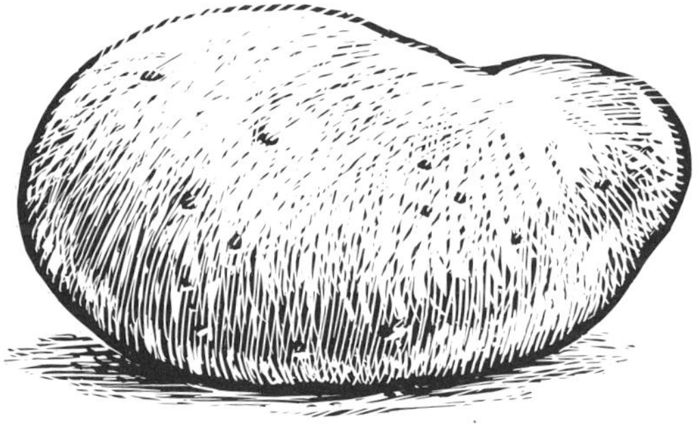

Basic Mash

Mashed potatoes are one of the classic comfort foods – creamy and satisfying. Mash is perfect with grilled sausages and onion gravy or on its own with melted butter. You should definitely use a floury potato to get the right texture which you just can't get with waxy varieties.

1. Wash and peel 1½ kg / 3lb 6oz floury potatoes and cut into even sized chunks
2. Put in a pan of salted water, cover and bring to the boil. Simmer until completely tender.
3. Drain and put back into the pan. Put back on the heat to drive off any excess water.
4. Season well, add 85g / 3oz butter and mash with a fork or a potato masher until completely smooth.

Garlic Mash

As for basic mash but add 5 peeled cloves of garlic to the potatoes at stage 1 and substitute the butter for 90ml / 3 fl oz olive oil.

Herby Mash

As for basic mash but add 6 tbsp chopped fresh mixed herbs (parsley, chives, thyme, marjoram, oregano) to the potatoes at stage 4 with plenty of black pepper and substitute the butter for 4 tbsp sour cream, crème fraiche or natural yoghurt.

Mustard Mash

As for basic mash but add 2 tbsp grain mustard to the potatoes at stage 4 and substitute the butter for 4 tbsp crème fraiche.

Olive Mash

As for basic mash but add 85g / 3oz chopped black olives and 2 tbsp chopped fresh basil to the potatoes at stage 4 and leave out the butter.

Potato and Celeriac Mash

1. Peel and cube 750g / 1½ lb floury potatoes and 750g / 1½ lb celeriac. Put in a pan of salted water and bring to the boil.
2. Drain and put back into the pan. Put back on the heat to drive off any excess water.
3. Season well, add 85g / 3oz butter and 85g / 3oz shredded spring onions. Mash with a fork or a potato masher until completely smooth.

Variations – substitute the celeriac for 750g / 1½ lb parsnips, swede or turnips.

Baked Potatoes

I think long, slow baking achieves the fluffiest baked potato with a crunchy skin.

1. Heat the oven to 190°C / 375°F / Gas 5.
2. Wash 6 large baking potatoes and prick all over with a fork or sharp knife.
3. Put in the oven and bake for 1½ - 2 hours until completely tender when pierced with a sharp knife or skewer.

Fillings:

These are some of my favourite fillings for baked potatoes although it takes a lot to beat butter and your favourite cheese with lots of black pepper.

Guacamole

1. Peel and stone 2 ripe avocados. Mash to a rough purée with a fork.
2. Stir in 2 deseeded, chopped, ripe tomatoes, 1 peeled and crushed clove of garlic, the juice of 1 lemon and 2 tbsp chopped fresh coriander. Season well and serve.

Hummus

1. Drain and rinse a 400g / 14oz tin chickpeas and put in a food processor with the juice of 1 lemon, 2-3 cloves peeled garlic, ½ tsp ground cumin, ½ tsp paprika, 2 tbsp light tahini and 4 tbsp olive oil.
2. Season well and whizz until smooth.

Braised Cabbage

1. Core and shred a small Savoy cabbage.
2. Heat 30ml / 2 tbsp olive oil and add 1 peeled and chopped onion, 1 peeled and crushed clove of garlic, 1 deveined, deseeded and finely chopped fresh red chilli and the cabbage. Season with salt and pepper.
3. Add 120ml / 4 fl oz vegetable stock. Cover and cook very slowly until the cabbage is very tender.

Coleslaw

1. Core and shred a small white cabbage. Peel and grate 2 large carrots. Core and grate 2 apples.
2. Mix the cabbage, carrots and apples together with 120g / 4oz mayonnaise, the zest and juice 1 lemon, 2 tbsp chopped fresh parsley, 60g / 2oz sultanas and 2 tbsp toasted sunflower seeds.

Purple Sprouting Broccoli with Parmesan

675g / 1½ lb	Purple sprouting broccoli
120g / 4oz	Freshly grated Parmesan
2	Cloves garlic, peeled and crushed
45ml / 3 tbsp	Olive oil
	Salt and pepper

1. Heat the oil in a large saucepan and add the broccoli and garlic. Turn the heat down to low, cover and cook very slowly until the broccoli is tender.
2. When the broccoli is tender, toss through the Parmesan and season well. Serve at once.

Stuffed Baked Potatoes

1. Bake 6 potatoes and when cooked cut in half and scrape the insides into a bowl. Season with salt and pepper.
2. Mix in 120g / 4oz crème fraiche, 3 tbsp chopped fresh mixed herbs and 1 bunch finely sliced spring onions.
3. Put on a baking sheet and bake in the oven (190°C / 375°F / Gas 5) for 20-30 minutes until the tops are golden and crunchy.

   Variations – add 120g / 4oz grated cheese or 120g / 4oz chopped cooked bacon.

Chips

I have to admit to rarely making chips traditionally as I find oven chips quicker and easier. Sometimes, however, only proper chips will do – usually with fried eggs or in-between 2 slices of thick, buttered white bread with plenty of tomato ketchup.

1. Peel 1½ kg / 3lb 6oz floury potatoes and cut lengthways into 1cm across chips. Wash in cold water to get rid of any starch and squeeze dry in a clean tea towel.
2. Pour sunflower oil into a large saucepan so that it is half full. Heat slowly until it is at 160°C / 320°F.
3. Blanch the chips in a chip basket in batches for 5-6 minutes until they become limp but not coloured. Drain well.
4. Raise the temperature of the oil to 190°C / 375°F and cook the chips, again in batches, for 3-4 minutes until golden brown and crispy. Drain on kitchen paper, sprinkle with salt and malt vinegar and serve at once.

Oven Chips

1. Heat the oven to 200°C / 400°F / Gas 6.
2. Scrub 1½ kg / 3lb 6oz floury potatoes and cut into even sized wedges.
3. Toss in 6 tbsp sunflower oil and put in a roasting tin in a single layer – you may have to put them in 2 tins.
4. Bake for 40-50 minutes, turning them with a fish slice from time to time.
5. When they are golden brown, crunchy on the outside and soft in the middle, sprinkle over a little salt and serve at once.

Roast Potatoes

Another classic way of enjoying potatoes, along with mash and chips. They are best made with floury potatoes to get a crunchy outside and creamy, melting inside. Make sure the fat is really hot before you put them in - goose or duck fat or dripping give a superior flavour but can be difficult to get hold of but olive oil works well too.

1. Wash and peel 1kg / 2¼ lb floury potatoes. Cut into even sized chunks. Put in a saucepan of salted water and bring to the boil. Cover and simmer until parboiled – about 5-8 minutes – so that the potatoes still resist a knife when it goes in.
2. Heat the oven to 220°C / 425°F / Gas 7. Put 120ml / 4 fl oz olive oil or 120g / 4oz goose or duck fat into a roasting tin and heat in the oven until very hot and smoking.
3. Drain the potatoes and toss together in a large sieve or colander to roughen the edges.
4. Put the roasting tin of hot fat on the hob and turn the heat on to low underneath – be careful to avoid splashes. Put the potatoes in the tin in a single layer and baste them with the fat.
5. Put back in the oven for 40-50 minutes turning from time to time until they are crunchy and golden on the outside and soft all the way through.

Spiced Roast Potatoes

As for roast potatoes but at stage 3, toss the potatoes in the following mixture – 2 tbsp tomato ketchup mixed with 2 tsp paprika,
1 tsp ground cumin, 2 tsp ground coriander and the zest and juice of
1 lemon.

Oven-Baked Potatoes with Rosemary and Garlic

1½ kg / 3lb 6oz	Potatoes, washed and cubed
6	Cloves garlic, peeled and crushed
3 tbsp	Very finely chopped fresh rosemary
120ml / 4 fl oz	Olive oil
	Salt and pepper

1. Heat the oven to 200°C / 400°F / Gas 6.
2. Mix the oil with the garlic and rosemary and toss with the potatoes.
3. Divide them between 2 roasting tins in a single layer and bake, turning from time to time, for 50 minutes, until crisp, golden brown and tender. Season with salt and pepper and serve.

Oven-Baked Potatoes with Lemon and Marjoram

1½ kg / 3lb 6oz	Potatoes, washed and cubed
3	Cloves garlic, peeled and roughly chopped
120ml / 4 fl oz	Olive oil
240ml / 8 fl oz	Chicken stock
	Juice and zest 2 lemons
4 tbsp	Chopped fresh marjoram

1. Heat the oven to 200°C / 400°F / Gas 6.
2. Toss the potatoes with the garlic and oil and put into 2 roasting tins. Bake in the oven for 30 minutes and divide the stock between the 2 trays. Bake for another 20 minutes.
3. Mix the juice and zest of 1 lemon and 2 tbsp chopped fresh marjoram into each tray with plenty of freshly ground black pepper. Bake for another 10 minutes. Sprinkle with salt and serve at once.

Colcannon

These recipes for colcannon, boxty and champ all come from my Irish grandfather's family; he was firmly of the opinion that a meal wasn't complete without potatoes.

750g / 1½ lb	Hot mashed potatoes
750g / 1½ lb	Hot cooked cabbage
1	Bunch spring onions, trimmed and shredded
180ml / 6 fl oz	Milk
120g / 4oz	Butter, cut into 6 cubes
	Salt and pepper

1. Put the onions in a small pan with the milk and cook until tender.
2. Mix the onions and milk into the mash and fold in the cabbage. Season well.
3. Divide the potato mixture into 6 and pile on to 6 plates. Put a cube of butter on to each mound and allow to melt. Serve at once. Delicious with grilled gammon steaks.

Boxty

These are perfect for brunch; try adding some freshly chopped parsley or chives or substitute the onion for shredded spring onions.

225g / 8oz	Potatoes, peeled and grated
225g / 8oz	Mashed potatoes
1	Onion, peeled and finely chopped
60g / 2oz	Plain flour
150ml / 5 fl oz	Milk
30ml / 2 tbsp	Sunflower oil
30g / 1oz	Butter
	Salt and pepper

1. Mix together the potatoes, mash, onion, flour and milk and season well.
2. Melt the oil and butter together in a large frying pan and when foaming add spoonfuls of the mixture. Fry gently until golden brown on both sides, drain on kitchen paper and serve straight away.

Champ

1½ kg / 3lb 6oz	Hot mashed potatoes
1	Bunch spring onions, trimmed and shredded
180ml / 6 fl oz	Milk
120g / 4oz	Butter, cut into 6 cubes
	Salt and pepper

1. Mix the onions and milk into the mash and season well.
2. Divide the potato mixture into 6 and pile on to 6 plates. Put a cube of butter on to each mound. Serve at once with the butter melting.

Bubble and Squeak

500g / 1lb 2 oz	Mashed potatoes
500g / 1lb 2 oz	Cooked cabbage
60g / 2oz	Butter
	Salt and pepper

1. Mix the potatoes with the cabbage and season well. Shape into a round cake 3cm deep and cut into 8 wedges.
2. Melt the butter in a large frying pan until foaming.
3. Fry the wedges on both sides until golden brown and crunchy and serve at once.

Rosti

750g / 1½ lb	Potatoes, peeled and grated
30g / 1oz	Butter
30ml / 2 tbsp	Olive oil
	Salt and pepper

1. Put the grated potato in a clean towel and squeeze out all the liquid. Season well.
2. Melt the butter and the oil together in a non-stick frying pan and when foaming, add the grated potatoes.
3. Cook gently until golden brown and slide the rosti on to a plate. Add a little more butter and oil to the pan if dry and return to the pan, cooked side up.
4. When the bottom is golden brown, cut the rosti into wedges and serve

Variations – mix the potatoes with other grated root vegetables such as celeriac, carrots, parsnips, swedes and turnips. You can also make individual rosti instead of 1 large one.

Sauté Potatoes

1½ kg / 3lb 6oz	Potatoes, peeled and cubed
120ml / 4 fl oz	Olive oil
	Salt and pepper

1. Heat the oil in 2 large frying pans and add the potatoes in a single layer. You may have to cook the potatoes in batches.
2. Cook very slowly turning the cubes when each side is crisp and golden until cooked on all sides. Season with salt and pepper and serve.

Potato Cakes

500g / 1lb 2oz	Cold mashed potatoes
85g / 3oz	Plain flour
60g / 2oz	Butter
	Salt and pepper

1. Mix the potatoes with the flour and season well.
2. Knead to a smooth dough and roll out until 2½cm / 1 inch thick. Cut into rounds and chill until needed
3. Melt the butter and when foaming, cook the potato cakes until golden brown on each side. Serve at once.

Gratin Dauphinois

1½kg / 3lb 6oz	Floury potatoes, peeled and sliced very thinly
3	Cloves garlic, peeled and crushed
600ml / 1 pint	Double cream
30g / 1oz	Butter
	Nutmeg
	Salt and pepper

1. Heat the oven to 170°C / 325°F / Gas 3.
2. In a shallow ovenproof dish, layer the potatoes with the garlic and season as you do so with freshly grated nutmeg, salt and pepper.
3. Pour the cream over the potatoes, dot the butter over the top and bake in the oven for 2 hours until tender and golden.

Potatoes Boulangère

1½kg / 3lb 6oz	Floury potatoes, washed and sliced very thinly
2	Onions, peeled and thinly sliced
3	Cloves garlic, peeled and crushed
600ml / 1 pint	Hot chicken stock
	Salt and pepper

1. Heat the oven to 170°C / 325°F / Gas 3.
2. In a shallow ovenproof dish, layer the potatoes with the onions and garlic and season as you do so.
3. Pour the stock over the potatoes, bake in the oven for 2 hours until tender and golden brown.

Lyonnais Potatoes

1½ kg / 3lb 6oz	Potatoes, peeled, parboiled and thickly sliced
4	Onions, peeled and finely sliced
120ml / 4 fl oz	Olive oil
	Salt and pepper

1. Heat the oil in 2 large frying pans and fry the potato slices until crisp and golden on each side.
2. When you turn the potatoes, add the onions and fry with the potatoes until soft and golden.
3. Season with salt and pepper and serve.

Potatoes with White Wine, Bacon and Thyme

1kg / 2lb 4oz	Waxy potatoes, washed and cubed
3	Red onions, peeled and sliced
2	Cloves garlic, peeled and crushed
120g / 4oz	Smoked, streaky bacon, derinded and chopped
2 tbsp	Fresh thyme leaves
150ml / 5 fl oz	Dry white wine
2 tbsp	Crème fraiche
15ml / 1 tbsp	Olive oil
	Salt and pepper

1. Heat the oil and add the onions, bacon and garlic. Cook for 2 minutes.
2. Add the potatoes, thyme and wine and season well. Cover and cook very gently for 15 minutes, stirring from time to time, until the potatoes are tender.
3. Stir in the crème fraiche and serve.

Potatoes with Tomatoes and Basil

1kg / 2lb 4oz	Waxy potatoes, washed and cubed
1	Bunch spring onions, trimmed and shredded
2	Cloves garlic, peeled and crushed
1 x 400g / 14oz	Tin chopped tomatoes
30ml / 2 tbsp	Balsamic vinegar
	Handful fresh basil, shredded
15ml / 1 tbsp	Olive oil
	Salt and pepper

1. Heat the oil and add the onions, tomatoes, garlic and balsamic vinegar. Season well.
2. Cook over a low heat until the tomatoes have broken down to form a thick sauce – about 15 minutes.
3. Add the potatoes and stir well. Cover and cook very gently until the potatoes are tender. Stir in the basil and serve.

Hot-Spiced Potatoes

$1\frac{1}{2}$ kg / 3lb 6oz	Small waxy potatoes, scrubbed and halved
6	Cloves garlic, peeled and crushed
1	Fresh red chilli, deseeded and deveined
2 tsp	Ground cumin
2 tsp	Ground coriander
2 tsp	Paprika
120ml / 4 fl oz	Red wine vinegar
120ml / 4 fl oz	Sunflower oil
3 tbsp	Freshly chopped parsley
	Salt and pepper

1. Boil the potatoes until tender and drain.
2. Whizz all the other ingredients together with a hand blender.
3. Toss over the potatoes whilst hot and serve at once.

Balsamic Potatoes with Bacon

1½ kg / 3lb 6oz	Waxy potatoes, washed and quartered
200g / 7oz	Smoked bacon, derinded and chopped
3	Red onions, peeled and sliced
90ml / 6 tbsp	Balsamic vinegar
3 tbsp	Freshly chopped parsley
	Salt and pepper

1. Heat the oven to 220°C / 425°F / Gas 7.
2. Parboil the potatoes for 5 minutes. Drain and shake dry. Mix with the bacon, onions and balsamic vinegar.
3. Turn into a roasting tin and bake in the oven for 30-40 minutes, turning from time to time.
4. Toss with the parsley and season with salt and pepper. Serve at once.

Chocolate Potato Cake

As this cake contains polenta and not wheat, it is good for those with wheat allergies. It is very moist and keeps well but you can also eat it hot as a pudding with ice cream.

Use a good quality chocolate and cocoa such as Green and Black's. I like to use their Maya Gold chocolate in this recipe for its delicious spicy flavour.

120g / 4oz	Mashed potatoes
180g / 6oz	Butter
225g / 8oz	Caster sugar
3	Eggs
120g / 4oz	Plain chocolate, melted
225g / 8oz	Fine polenta / cornmeal
30g / 1oz	Cocoa

1. Heat the oven to 180°C / 350°F / Gas 4. Grease and line a 25cm / 10 inch cake tin.
2. Cream the butter, potato and sugar until light and fluffy. Beat in the eggs. Stir in the melted chocolate.
3. Fold in the polenta and cocoa and turn the mixture into the cake tin.
4. Cook for 30-40 minutes until an inserted skewer comes out cleanly.

If you want a topping for this cake, gently melt together 60g / 2oz butter with 85g / 3oz dark chocolate. Mix together until glossy and let the mixture to cool until it thickens slightly. Pour over the cake until just set and shave over some white chocolate with a potato peeler.

Potato and Orange Cake

2	Oranges
180g / 6oz	Butter
180g / 6oz	Caster sugar
3	Eggs
120g / 4oz	Mashed potato
180g / 6oz	Self-raising flour

1. Put the oranges in a pan and cover with water. Bring to the boil and simmer until soft. Quarter and deseed the oranges and whizz until smooth in a food processor. Cool.
2. Heat the oven to 180°C / 350°F / Gas 4. Line a loose-bottomed 25cm / 10 inch cake tin with baking parchment.
3. Cream the butter and the sugar until pale and creamy. Beat in the eggs. Fold in the oranges, mashed potato and flour.
4. Turn into the cake tin and bake in the oven for 40 minutes until golden brown and an inserted skewer comes out clean.

Ginger and Potato Cake

180g / 6oz	Butter
180g / 6oz	Caster sugar
3	Eggs
180g / 6oz	Self-raising flour
30g / 1oz	Black treacle
2 tsp	Ground ginger
150g / 5oz	Grated potato

1. Heat the oven to 180˚C / 350˚F / Gas 4. Line a 20cm / 8 inch loose-bottomed cake tin with baking parchment.
2. Cream the butter and the sugar together. Beat in the eggs and the treacle.
3. Fold the flour into the cake mix with the ground ginger and grated potato. Turn into the tin and bake in the oven for 50-60 minutes until an inserted skewer comes out clean.

Potato Scones

450g / 1lb	Mashed potatoes
60g / 2oz	Butter, melted
60g / 2oz	Caster sugar
	Pinch of salt
120g / 4oz	Sultanas
225g / 8oz	Self-raising flour

1. Heat the oven to 220°C / 425°F / Gas 7.
2. Mix the potatoes with the sugar, salt, sultanas and melted butter. Stir in the flour to make a stiff dough.
3. Shape into a round 2½cm / 1 inch thick and put on a baking tray. Mark into 8-10 segments and bake for 30 minutes until golden brown and crusty.
4. Cool on a wire rack for 10 minutes and serve warm with butter and preserves. Also good toasted the next day.

Cheesy Potato Scones

You can use any hard cheese for this – whichever is your favourite: Cheddar, Lancashire, Cheshire, Double Gloucester, Parmesan ... Makes 8 scones.

180g / 6oz	Self-raising flour
60g / 2oz	Butter
	Pinch salt
120g / 4oz	Mashed potatoes
85g / 3oz	Good flavoured cheese, grated
60ml / 2 fl oz	Milk

1. Heat the oven to 220°C / 425°F / Gas 7.
2. Rub the butter into the flour and stir in the salt, cheese and potatoes.
3. Add enough milk to make a soft but not sticky dough.
4. Knead lightly and pat out to a 2½cm / 1 inch deep round.
5. Cut into rounds and put on a baking tray. Bake for 12-15 minutes until golden and risen.

Variations – instead of cheese you could add fresh chopped herbs, chopped cooked bacon, cooked leeks or onions.

Sarah's Pasties

This is Sarah Beardsmore's recipe from the Organic Farm Shop, Cirencester. These pasties are so good that they were highly commended at the 2000 Organic Food Awards.

450g / 1lb	Plain flour
225g / 8oz	Butter
450g / 1lb	Leeks, trimmed, washed and sliced
450g / 1lb	Potatoes, peeled and cubed
200g / 7oz	Mature Cheddar cheese, grated
1	Beaten egg
	Salt and pepper

1. Rub the butter into the flour and add only enough water to bind it into pastry. Roll the pastry out and, using a 20cm / 8 inch plate, cut out 6 circles.
2. Steam the potatoes and leeks separately until tender. Cool.
3. Gently mix together the leeks, potatoes and cheese and add some salt and pepper.
4. Divide the mixture between the 6 circles. Brush the edges of the pastry with the beaten egg and seal together to make pasties. Brush the outsides of the pasties with the rest of the beaten egg. Put on a baking sheet and chill for 30 minutes.
5. Heat the oven to 200°C / 400°F / Gas 6. Bake the pasties for 30 minutes until the pastry is cooked and golden. Serve hot or at room temperature.

Potato Pastry

This is a very light pastry.

120g / 4oz	Plain flour
120g / 4oz	Mashed potato
85g / 3oz	Butter
	Pinch of salt

1. Stir the salt into the flour and rub in the butter.
2. Add the potatoes and knead to make a soft dough.
3. Chill the pastry in the fridge for 30 minutes before using it.
4. Roll out the pastry and use as required.

Layered Potato Pie

1½ quantity	Potato pastry recipe
600g / 1lb 5oz	Boiled potatoes, sliced
280g / 10oz	Leeks, trimmed, washed and sliced
450g / 1lb	Squash, peeled and cubed
3 tbsp	Fresh chopped parsley
300ml / ½ pint	Milk
30g / 1oz	Butter
30g / 1oz	Plain flour
120g / 4oz	Mature Cheddar, grated
1	Beaten egg
	Salt and pepper

1. Steam the leeks and squash until tender. Cool.
2. Melt the butter in a saucepan and stir in the flour. Cook for 2 minutes and, off the heat, stir in half the milk until smooth. Stir in the rest of the milk and bring to the boil, stirring all the time. Simmer gently for 10 minutes, stirring from time to time. Season well, stir in the parsley, cheese, leeks and squash. Cool.
3. Roll out ¾ of the pastry and use to line a deep, loose-bottomed, 20cm / 8 inch cake tin. Layer the potatoes with the vegetable mixture, finishing with a layer of potatoes.
4. Roll out the rest of the pastry and use it to make a lid. Seal and brush it with the beaten egg and cut a steam hole in the centre. Chill for 30 minutes.
5. Heat the oven to 200°C / 400°F / Gas 6. Bake the pie for 50 minutes until the pastry is golden brown and the filling is piping hot.

Creamy Leek, Ham and Potato Tart

1 quantity	Potato pastry recipe
4	Leeks, trimmed, sliced and washed
340g / 12oz	Waxy potatoes, washed and cubed
225g / 8oz	Cooked ham, shredded
600ml / 1 pint	Milk
30g / 1oz	Butter
30g / 1oz	Plain flour
1 tbsp	Fresh finely chopped rosemary
1 tsp	Grain mustard
3	Eggs
	Salt and pepper

1. Heat the oven to 200°C / 400°F / Gas 6.
2. Roll out the pastry to line a 25cm / 10 inch tart tin and chill in the fridge for 20 minutes. Line with greaseproof paper and baking beans and bake in the oven for 15 minutes until the sides have set and the base has dried out. (Take the paper and beans out after 10 minutes to let the base dry out). Reduce the heat to 180°C / 350°F / Gas 4.
3. Boil the potatoes until tender, drain and cool. Steam the leeks until tender and cool.
4. Melt the butter in a saucepan and stir in the flour. Cook for 2 minutes and, off the heat, stir in the milk. Put back on the heat and, stirring all the time, bring to the boil. Simmer gently for 10 minutes, stirring from time to time.
5. Beat in the eggs, rosemary and mustard and season well. Stir in the potatoes, ham and leeks and turn into the pastry case.
6. Bake in the oven for 30 minutes until the tart is set and the top is golden.

Red Pepper, Leek and Potato Tart

1 quantity	Potato pastry recipe
1	Large red pepper, seeded and thinly sliced
200g / 7oz	Leeks, trimmed, washed and sliced
280g / 10oz	Waxy potatoes, washed and finely diced
150g / 5oz	Crème fraiche
3	Eggs
1 tbsp	Chopped fresh chives
15ml / 1 tbsp	Olive oil

1. Heat the oven to 200°C / 400°F / Gas 6.
2. Roll out the pastry to line a 25cm / 10 inch tart tin and chill in the fridge for 20 minutes. Line with greaseproof paper and baking beans and bake in the oven for 15 minutes until the sides have set and the base has dried out. (Take the paper and beans out after 10 minutes to let the base dry out). Reduce the heat to 180°C / 350°F / Gas 4.
3. Heat the oil in a saucepan and add the red pepper, leeks and potatoes. Cover and cook very gently until the potatoes are tender. Season and turn into the pastry case.
4. Mix the crème fraiche with the eggs and chives and pour over the potato mixture. Bake in the oven for 30 minutes or until set and golden. Serve hot or at room temperature.

Trout and Potato Tart with Chives and Spring Onions

1 quantity	Potato pastry recipe
280g / 10oz	Waxy potatoes, peeled, cubed and cooked
2	Trout
1	Bunch spring onions, trimmed and sliced
2 tbsp	Finely chopped fresh chives
200g / 7oz	Crème fraiche
3	Eggs
	Salt and pepper

1. Heat the oven to 200˚C / 400˚F / Gas 6.
2. Roll out the pastry to line a 25cm / 10 inch tart tin and chill in the fridge for 20 minutes. Line with greaseproof paper and baking beans and bake in the oven for 15 minutes until the sides have set and the base has dried out. (Take the paper and beans out after 10 minutes to let the base dry out).
3. Put the trout in the oven at the same time and bake for 15 minutes. Cool slightly. Skin and bone the fish and break the flesh into large flakes. Turn the oven temperature down to 180˚C / 350˚F / Gas 4.
4. Gently mix the fish with the potatoes, spring onions and chives and turn into the pastry case. Beat the eggs with the crème fraiche and season well. Pour over the mixture in the case.
5. Bake in the oven for 30 minutes until the tart is set and lightly golden.

Potato Pie with Garlic and Herbs

450g / 1lb	Waxy potatoes
6	Cloves garlic, peeled and crushed
2 tbsp	Chopped fresh parsley
1 tbsp	Chopped fresh chives
1 tbsp	Chopped fresh thyme
1 quantity	Potato pastry recipe
120g / 4oz	Crème fraiche
1	Egg, beaten
	Salt and pepper

1. Heat the oven to 200°C / 400°F / Gas 6.
2. Parboil the potatoes. Cool, peel and slice thinly.
3. Mix the herbs and garlic into the crème fraiche and season well. Toss the potato slices in the herby mixture and turn into a 25cm / 10 inch flan dish. Roll out the pastry to make a lid. Place over the potatoes and cut an air hole in the centre. Glaze with beaten egg.
4. Bake in the oven for 30 minutes until the pastry is golden.

Potato and Fennel Pie

1 quantity	Potato pastry recipe
15ml / 1 tbsp	Olive oil
280g / 10oz	Bulb fennel, trimmed and sliced
280g / 10oz	Orange fleshed sweet potatoes, peeled and cubed
450g / 1lb	Waxy potatoes, washed and cubed
30g / 1oz	Butter
30g / 1oz	Plain flour
300ml / ½ pint	Milk
1 tbsp	Fresh rosemary, chopped
2 tbsp	Chopped fresh parsley
60g / 2oz	Parmesan cheese, grated
	Salt and pepper

1. Heat the oven to 200°C / 400°F / Gas 6.
2. Heat the oil and gently cook the fennel in it. Boil the sweet potato and potato until tender and drain.
3. Melt the butter in a saucepan and stir in the flour. Cook for 2 minutes and, off the heat, stir in the milk until smooth. Put back on the heat and bring to the boil, stirring all the time. Simmer gently for 10 minutes, stirring from time to time. Season well, stir in the potato, sweet potato, fennel, parsley, rosemary and Parmesan. Cool.
4. Put into a 25cm / 10 inch flan dish and roll out the pastry to make a lid. Seal, glaze with a little beaten egg and cut an air hole in the centre. Bake in the oven for 30 minutes until the pastry is cooked and golden and the filling hot.

Potato and Pea Parcels

450g / 1lb	Potatoes, peeled and cubed
225g / 8oz	Frozen peas
1	Onion, peeled and thinly sliced
1	Clove garlic, peeled and crushed
15ml / 1 tbsp	Sunflower oil
½ tsp	Turmeric
1 tsp	Ground coriander
½ tsp	Ground cumin
1 tsp	Paprika
2 tbsp	Chopped fresh mint
Double quantity	Potato pastry recipe
1	Egg, beaten

1. Heat the oil and add the onion, potatoes, frozen peas and garlic. Stir and add the spices and season well. Cover and cook gently for 15 minutes until the potatoes are tender. Cool and stir in the mint.
2. Roll out the pastry and cut out twelve 10cm / 4 inch squares. Put 2 tbsp of the potato mix on each pastry square. Brush the edges with the beaten egg and fold the pastry over to make triangles, sealing the edges as you do so.
3. Put on a baking sheet and chill for 20 minutes. Brush the parcels with more beaten egg and bake for 15-20 minutes in a hot oven - 200°C / 400°F / Gas 6. Serve hot or at room temperature.

Potato and Polenta Bread

500g / 1lb 2oz	Smooth mashed potato
500g / 1lb 2oz	Strong white flour
180g / 6oz	Fine polenta
15g / ½oz	Fresh yeast
1	Egg
1 tsp	Salt
60g / 2oz	Melted butter, cooled
300ml / 10 fl oz	Lukewarm milk

1. Heat the oven to 220°C / 425°F / Gas 7.
2. Mix the yeast with a little of the milk. Mix the flour, polenta, salt, potato, egg, butter and yeast liquid together and add the rest of the milk. Mix together to make a soft but not sticky dough.
3. Knead for 10 minutes until smooth and elastic. Put in a clean bowl, cover and leave in a warm place until the dough is well-risen – about 1 hour.
4. Heat the oven to 220°C / 425°F / Gas 7.
5. Knead the dough for another 5 minutes. Shape into 12-16 rolls and put on a lightly greased baking sheet. Cover and leave to rise for 15 minutes.
6. Glaze with a little extra milk and sprinkle with a little extra polenta. Bake in the oven for 15 minutes until they are well-risen and golden and sound hollow when tapped on their base. Cool on a wire rack.

Potato, Spinach and Sweet Potato Rolls

340g / 12oz	Waxy potatoes, peeled and cubed
340g / 12oz	Orange sweet potatoes, peeled and cubed
450g / 1lb	Spinach, washed
300ml / ½ pint	Milk
30g / 1oz	Butter
30g / 1oz	Plain flour
	Whole nutmeg
1 quantity	Potato pastry recipe
1	Egg, beaten
	Salt and pepper

1. Cook the spinach until it wilts, squeeze out any excess water and cool. Only cook it in the water that clings to the leaves after washing and draining.
2. Boil the potato and sweet potato until tender. Drain and cool.
3. Melt the butter in a saucepan and stir in the flour. Cook for 2 minutes and, off the heat, stir in the milk. Put back on the heat and, stirring all the time, bring to the boil. Simmer gently for 10 minutes, stirring from time to time. Season and add a little grated whole nutmeg. Cool.
4. Mix the spinach, potato and sweet potato into the sauce. Roll out the pastry to 2 rectangles 30cm / 12 inches / 6 inches. Divide the spinach mixture between the 2 rectangles and form a long sausage with it down the centre of the pastry. Brush the edges with beaten egg and seal the 2 long sides together. Cut into 10cm / 4 inch rolls and put on a baking sheet. Chill in the fridge for 30 minutes.
5. Heat the oven to 200°C / 400°F / Gas 6. Brush the rolls with the rest of the beaten egg and bake in the oven for 25-30 minutes until the pastry is cooked and golden.
6. Serve hot or at room temperature. You could make smaller rolls for parties.

Spiced Pumpkin and Potato Bread

500g / 1lb 2oz	Strong white flour
180g / 6oz	Smooth mashed potato
180g / 6oz	Cooked pumpkin, mashed
15g / ½oz	Fresh yeast
30ml / 2 tbsp	Sunflower oil
1 tsp	Salt
1 tsp	Ground ginger
1 tsp	Ground cinnamon
200ml / 7 fl oz	Lukewarm water
120g / 4oz	Pumpkin seeds, toasted

1. Mix the yeast with a little of the water. Mix the flour, salt, pumpkin, potato, spices, oil and yeast liquid together and add the rest of the water. Mix together to make a soft but not sticky dough.
2. Knead for 10 minutes until smooth and elastic. Put in a clean bowl, cover and leave in a warm place until the dough is well-risen – about 1 hour.
3. Heat the oven to 220°C / 425°F / Gas 7.
4. Knead the dough for another 5 minutes, working in the pumpkin seeds as you do so. Shape into 2 round loaves and put on a lightly greased baking sheet. Cover and leave to rise for 15 minutes.
5. Bake in the oven for 30-40 minutes until the loaf is well risen and golden and sounds hollow when tapped on its base.
6. Cool on a wire rack and serve with preserves for breakfast or tea. Delicious toasted.

Potato and Herb Bread

225g / 8oz	Smooth mashed potatoes
15g / ½oz	Fresh yeast
300ml / 10 fl oz	Handhot water
30ml / 2 tbsp	Olive oil
2 tbsp	Mixed chopped fresh herbs – rosemary, thyme, parsley, chives, marjoram
1 tsp	Salt
600g / 1lb 5oz	Strong white flour

1. Mix the yeast with a little of the water.
2. Mix together the potato, herbs, yeast mixture, flour and salt to make a soft dough with the rest of the water.
3. Turn on to a work surface and knead for 10 minutes until smooth and elastic.
4. Put into a clean bowl, cover and leave in a warm place until well-risen and puffy - about 1 hour.
5. Knock back the dough and shape into a loaf. Place on a baking sheet, cover and leave to prove for about 10-15 minutes.
6. Bake in a hot oven – 220˚C / 425˚F / Gas 7 - until risen and crusty – about 40 minutes.

Variations – at stage 5, you could add cooked onions or leeks, chopped olives or sundried tomatoes, or grated cheese.

- Growing Potatoes Organically

- Potato Varieties

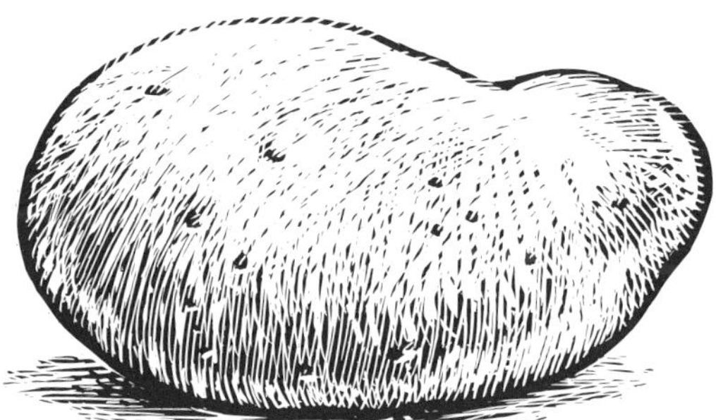

Growing Potatoes Organically in Gardens and on Allotments

Organic growing centres upon the health of the soil and the level of biodiversity in and around the plot. Organic gardeners assess soil health by the level of activity seen in the soil after the use of cover crops, manures, rotations, protection and timely cultivations. The importance of creating a balanced environment for plant growth cannot be overstressed; those in small gardens and allotments need to consider how best to achieve this.

Soil fertility is provided naturally and this area will be the most significant challenge when changing from standard potato production to the organic option. Too much nitrogen is just as bad as too little and the tradition of buying the annual load of manure may not be the panacea we think. We need to think about exactly what we are bringing into the garden and in what state.

For most gardeners (organic and conventional), the external influences will have a dramatic effect . This is best seen on allotments, where one untidy plot of weeds and potatoes growing from those left in the ground from last season will act as a base for slugs and blight spores to challenge the best organic gardeners.

If you want to read the organic standards, the Soil Association readily sells copies but they are aimed at commercial production. Instead, a visit to HDRA's organic gardens at Ryton, Yalding and Audley End should be enough to fascinate and enthuse the organically interested. And of course the annual HDRA Potato Day at Ryton Gardens puts the icing on the cake for the season to come.

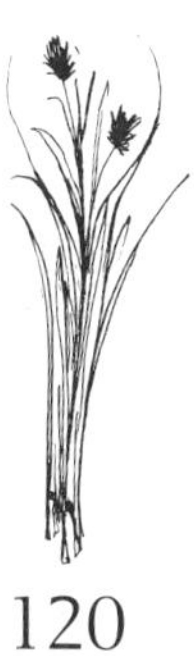

Where to Grow Organic Potatoes

The wonderful thing about the potato is that you can grow it in so many places and for so much of the year. A conservatory or greenhouse for early and late plantings, flower borders, allotments, vegetable patches, patios, roof gardens, on the coast, inland. If you have light, moderate warmth and are free from frost, you can grow potatoes.

Potatoes will grow in a wide range of soil types but they must be easily drained and not prone to flooding. Avoid shade as it encourages leggy plants. The usual rules apply:

- Lighten heavy clays and compacted soils by the addition of fine compost and double digging.
- Avoid acidic soils.
- Strengthen a sandy soil with organic material and provide protection by cover crops or any organic materials (or mats) that stop the goodness leaching out during the winter.

The work to produce a good organic potato is in the planning. Returning grassland back into production will provide welcome residual organic nutrition but also pests like wireworm. A vegetable patch will need that same nutrition added over winter and/or from a previous nitrogen-fixing crop like legumes.

Soils For Organic Potatoes

For most gardeners the type of soil is not the main reason for buying a house (but there are always exceptions!) so your soil cannot be chosen. Over the years you can condition it to some sort of perfection.

Light sandy soils are best for early crops, warming up quickly and allowing rapid growth, but they do dry out quickly. For maincrop potatoes, sandy soils are perfectly workable but it may be difficult to retain nutrition and moisture content.

Medium to heavy loam soils retain moisture and warm up later. It can be difficult to harvest potatoes from them if they have not been thoroughly prepared by digging.

Heavier clays can produce good crops but water retention and cracking in dry weather remain challenges.

Heavier soils, including some well-watered peats, tend to lower the dry matter percentage of your potato harvest. There are pluses and minuses to this, making floury varieties creamier and some creamy varieties wet.

A silt, limestone or loam soil will give a broad balance of yield, good texture and flavour.

Buying Seed Potatoes

The variety, quality, choice and availability of good potato seed has improved over recent years but you still need to keep a watchful eye when buying. During the winter you will have decided what varieties you need and identified your likely source.

The mail order companies publish catalogues in the autumn. Their range is good and you should order early for delivery after Christmas, but beware of substitutions.

Garden centres receive their stocks from mid to late January and you should purchase seed potatoes then, rather than in the spring.

HDRA Potato Day at Ryton Gardens is held on the first weekend in February and is an excellent source if you want small quantities and a wide choice.

Things to bear in mind when buying seed potatoes –

- Always buy good quality, certified seed.
- Be fussy when buying seed and try to get an even egg size with little or no damage to the tuber.
- Avoid seed tubers with any form of rot or dark patches around the stolon (rear end) of the tuber – this might be latent blackleg. If you see this or any other rot, walk away; don't take a chance.
- Avoid samples with white spindly sprouts.

Chitting Potatoes

- Once unpacked, stand the seed potatoes with the rose end (eyes) upwards in a shallow box or seed tray.
- Place in a light, dry, airy and frost-free place. This will encourage the eyes to open and form robust sturdy sprouts. Do this in January / February and by March the earlies will be ready, with the rest ready for April planting.
- If the tubers are shy in sprouting a little watering may help.
- Keep a close eye on temperatures as the seed tubers don't like being too warm (optimum temperature is 6-12°C).
- Look out for aphid movement and move to a cooler location if you suspect any.
- A slow-forming sprout will be much stronger than one that develops rapidly. Once your sprout is about 1cm long, the seed potato is ready for planting.

Planting Potatoes

Potatoes start to grow when the soil temperature has warmed up to 8°C and daytime temperatures are 10°C. Optimum development of the tuber will be around 15-18°C.

Tubers will grow at colder temperatures but they may develop a fault known as "little potato". These are small potatoes in which the solanine has built up creating a bitter taste - do not eat them.

If you want an early outside crop, planting in February or early March, you need to have an action plan in case of frost. In the early stages of growth this can be drawing earth over the crop but as the plant develops so the risk exacerbates. Be warned - don't plant too early.

Once the soil is suitable for digging, prepare a clod-free, well-drained and friable site. If you are returning from grassland, open the site as early as possible and turn over several times to control wireworm.

Manure may be dug in in the autumn for heavy soils or in the spring for light soils but be careful. Ensure the manure is well rotted, ideally with no straw and definitely no smell. Avoid intensive pig or cattle manure due to possible antibiotic risk . An ideal scenario is manure from an organic holding or a known horse manure supply. Watch out for weed germination.

Incorporate home produced compost and rake to a fine tilth. Plant tubers for new potatoes in rows 26 inches / 65cm apart, 4 inches / 10cm deep and 8 inches / 20cm apart in the row.

Stagger your planting according to your weekly needs by keeping the seed in the fridge for planting after April. Let's say you need 10lb / 4½ kg of new potatoes a week from June to August then plant 5 / 6 tubers fortnightly from early March through to late May. Apart from being logical and giving you the best condition for sweet, new potatoes, you will reduce your frost and blight risk.

Potatoes for maincrop (autumn and winter use) including second earlies should all be planted between late March and the end of May in maturity succession. Plant tubers for maincrop in rows 30-36 inches / 90-105cm apart, 6 inches / 15cm deep and 12 inches / 30cm apart in the rows.

Tubers for new potatoes can be planted into containers as small as 10 inches / 25cm deep and 9 inches / 22½cm wide. Select your strongest compost and ensure a constant water supply as the container is likely to dry out. Feed with homemade nutrient (comfrey, liquid manure) until foliage turns light green and show signs of dying back. This is an excellent method of growing for showing the potatoes in competition or if you're short of space. For the best results, the compost should be high quality and you may need to water daily.

New potatoes for Christmas can be planted 15 / 16 weeks before in containers or where frost protection can be afforded. Blight and other devastating fungal conditions will pose more of a problem to the possibly slow-growing, light-starved plants. For best results, plant as early as September.

Managing Your Organic Potato Crop

Organic gardeners know that the secret of a healthy crop lies in the soil but once planted, the management of the crop is just as important so you don't encourage disease or ruin cooking quality and flavour.

Once the young plants are through and a few inches high, you can earth up - drawing up the soil to protect plants from frost and tubers from greening. However this is not always necessary on raised beds or if the soil is going to be given a mulch. Both systems have merits.

The important point is (weather permitting) the control of the amount of water available to the plant. Increase the water to the young potato plant and you encourage more to set. This is good if you want a crop of medium sized tubers so long as sufficient nitrogen, potassium and potash (NPK) are available to develop the crop. If, like me, you are always short of the essential nutrients, you may choose not to water the young plants unless growth is impaired.

Once the plant is above 12 inches / 30cm then watering is essential and the timing is crucial. Water should be applied by trickle or around the plant base in the early hours of the morning. Watch the weather forecasts and if showers or rain are due, do not water.

Once the plant is fully-grown and begins to turn light green or yellow, stop watering and let the plant die down naturally. Don't be tempted to cut the stems back as this will inhibit flavour and spread disease.

Potato Pests

The management of the crop to its final conclusion is a constant assessment of risk. There are many pests and diseases that also like potatoes.

The **potato cyst nematode** (PCN) is the most damaging pest to the keen potato gardener and once established renders potato growing useless. For commercial growers it is the most worrying pest. It thrives on sucking the life out of the roots of plants. An almost microscopic nematode can lay thousands of cysts of which many survive and live in the soil on old rogue potatoes or other solanum species.

How do you know if you have PCN? Your plants will look stunted and underdeveloped, mature early and yield small tubers. If you pull up a plant, you may see the yellow or white cysts.

The white is pallida (P) strain and the yellow rostochiensis (R). There are many potato varieties available with good resistance to P but R is more of a problem and sadly more prevalent.

The non-chemical actions you can take include:

- Planting resistant or tolerant varieties.
- Trap-cropping (plant an early, resistant variety and harvest early, destroying all foliage off site).
- Long rotations: for prevention 1 year in 5; for partial cure 1 year in 10.
- Plant antagonistic crops like marigolds.
- Grow on heavier soils if possible.
- Use certified seed only.

If you are convinced you have a PCN infestation then you should grow only early varieties with resistance. After 5 / 6 years you will notice a dramatic fall in the infestation and be able to move back to a limited choice of second earlies and maincrops.

Slugs cause havoc to mature potato crops.

- You can control them by removing the over-wintering and breeding locations.
- Slugs and snails love the damp, wet undersides of wood, grass verges and hedge bases and these areas need to be kept tidy. Slugs will only come into your potato plot if you make it attractive for them so get rid of any long straggly foliage.
- Encourage slugs into beer traps around the plot to assess the population level.
- Visit the garden after an evening shower and pick up any slugs on the move.
- Potato varieties vary enormously in their slug susceptibility. When the crop is ready for harvest, dig them out and store them, rather than leaving them as food for slugs.
- Encourage hedgehogs, and if possible, let chickens run on the plot before and after planting.

Wireworm should only be a problem when digging up long-term grassland. This should be done in the autumn to expose the wireworms to birds and predators. If this pest is a problem after the first season then the land will need further cultivation to reduce its level.

Aphids will attack the foliage and suck the life out of leaves. They carry a virus which will reduce yields but it is rare for potato crops in the garden to suffer yield-affecting aphid damage. Ladybirds and other insects will control aphids so encourage them into the garden.

Colorado Beetle looks like the size of a ladybird but its striped lines make it distinctively different. It is a reportable pest and if established will devour potato crops.

Cutworms are chubby cream bugs about 1 inch / 2$^1/_2$ cm in length that visit the soil in dry conditions. Unlike slugs they focus on one potato and eat 50% of it rather then ploughing their way through small sections of many. You probably cause more damage when spearing the tubers with the fork when harvesting than is caused by the cutworm.

Potato Diseases

Phytophthora infestans is best known as blight and comes in various forms - leaf, stem and tuber; early and late. If present in high populations, the fungus will render the crop useless by rotting both the foliage and tuber. The first signs are blackened leaves or stems after rain or periods of high humidity.

Commercial conventional growers routinely spray against blight attack and on the whole the modern systemic blight sprays are efficient. However, they are not permitted under organic rules. Organic wisdom permits copper sulphate, which has far less efficacy and is highly persistent in the soil.

In keeping with organic principles, we must deal with blight on a preventative basis.

- Firstly the crop needs to be reasonably isolated and not next to an unkempt potato patch or dump of old tubers. Those growing on allotments will have a more difficult challenge as the weakest allotment holder will be your most likely source of the inoculum.
- Site your plot in a well-drained, open, non-shaded area.
- Keep nitrogen inputs to the minimum needed.
- Use healthy seed.
- Stagger planting.
- Water in the early morning and around the plant base if possible.
- Earth up plants and space widely between and in rows.

All good practice but if it rains and the leaves remain wet for 72 hours or more then blight conditions are at their highest. This is most likely in July and August.

Let's assume we are in a blight period. Is there anything to do apart from hope?

- Some growers recommend adding lemon juice to the water which lowers the pH on the leaf. This could work but is not proven.
- Use built-in variety resistance if you are prone to blight attacks. This will be worse in dense potato growing areas.
- Tuber blight is again variety prone and will be worse in wet conditions on poorly drained soils.
- Dry the tubers before storing.

Erwinia carotovora is a bacterium more commonly known as blackleg. It will probably come into your garden on diseased seed potatoes. Wet conditions encourage it and there is no control. Recognition of the disease is perhaps only a stem on one plant becoming shriveled and contracted. Look down at the stem base and you will see the black and smelly infection in full. Lift all infected plants and their tubers and destroy them. This disease although annoying is not in the same crop-disruptive class as blight. Good seed growing has reduced this problem significantly.

Streptomyces scabies (common scab) affects the look of the tubers and if widespread will shorten storage life. If you want to see scab in its full glory, grow a susceptible variety like Maris Piper. You can also encourage scab development by allowing the ground to become short of moisture at tuber initiation. Add water early if growing a susceptible variety or growing on a light soil.

Rhizoctonia solani (black scurf) is a commercial problem which should not bother the organic gardener unless the rotation is shortened. The classic symptoms seen on the tuber are black marks or growths distorting the cleanliness of the skin on a crop of reduced yield.

There are a number of other diseases, which can strike down potato crops but although serious in a worldwide context they are not established in the UK. However, failure to respect the rotational aspect of potato production will inevitably lead to a less sustainable potato growing plot.

Potential Problems

Viruses - There are a number of viruses that affect the potato crop some or all of which lead to yield reduction and some of which distort the internal and external aspects of the tuber. Spraing affects the tuber by creating circular lines in the inside of the flesh. Other viruses will curl and even destroy leaves. The good news is that today's seed industry has largely controlled potato viruses and if you purchase new certified seed, they should not be a problem.

Frost - is a major cause of poor yields and in recent year it seems that frost has not respected the global warming argument. The frustrating thing is that frost can be avoided by simple protection. Fleece absorbs one or two degrees below freezing. Its effect is to burn back leaves and stems. The plant will recover depending on foliage advancement but the number of tubers will be reduced. Some varieties make a poor recovery from frost.

Hollow Heart - is a common and avoidable problem easily recognized by a pit or hole in the centre of the tuber. It follows a period of dry weather followed by rain and favourable growing conditions. To a degree, it is variety prone as the types that make large tubers in mid-summer are most affected. It also causes splitting of the tuber skin.

Greening - Green potatoes are poisonous and therefore it is essential to ensure tubers are covered by soil. Earthing up the rows is the usual prevention. You also need to store potatoes in the dark.

Harvesting Your Organic Potatoes

Potatoes intended to be eaten as sweet fluffy-skinned new potatoes should be harvested when the plant is green and has been in full flower for a week. There is no exact science but counting the days of growth set against seasonal average temperatures is a good guide. A more traditional method is to scratch the soil away and look before digging.

Using a potato fork, enter the soil under the plant side-on and at an angle of 45 degrees, ease up the plant. If you want to capture that special freshly-dug aroma then cook within the next couple of hours.

Maincrops are an altogether different story. Let the haulms die back naturally and then dig in the same way. Work on the theory that the potatoes are best out of the soil if you are prone to slugs. There is little point in waiting for the plant to die if you have inadvertently over-used nitrogen and the crop will not die back. Again, check the yield. If you are satisfied then cut back the haulms to 2 inches / 5cm above the ground and leave for ten days for the skins to set. Don't harvest maincrop potatoes for winter storage with loose skins as they will brown and may turn soft. Destroy roots and foliage; do not compost them.

Choose a dry day for harvesting maincrop potatoes and let them dry before storage. Place them in paper or hessian sacks and store in a dark frost-free ventilated place such as a garage or shed.

If you have a large quantity of tubers, then you can make a potato clamp for storage. Place the tubers in a ridge on the soil surface. Cover with straw, to a depth of 6 inches / 15cm. Dig a trench around the potatoes and straw and place enough soil on the straw to hold it in position. Allow the potatoes to sweat (cure) for a week and then cover with 6 inches / 15cm of soil for frost protection. Leave a twist of straw exposed every 4 feet / 1.2m for ventilation. This method of storing potatoes was commonly used in really cold winters but for the average gardener, it is quite cumbersome.

Potato Varieties

The Potato Reference Collection at East Craigs houses over 1000 varieties but only about 60 of these are seriously grown in the UK commercially. About 10 potatoes dominate the UK commercial landscape and the average consumer can name only 1 variety - King Edward.

It became clear in the seventies and eighties that many well known varieties such as Great Scot, Eclipse, Redskin, Doon Star and Ninetyfold were being removed from the list, reducing choice. The final straw came when the EEC proposed that King Edward should not be sold because of its susceptibility to wart disease. British consumers were faced with losing the one variety they recognised.

The mission to raise potato variety awareness was highlighted in the 1970's by the founder of HDRA, Lawrence D Hills. Subsequently, several members of HDRA and the supermarket chain Waitrose have taken this up and it is why Jackie Gear started the annual Potato Day at Ryton Gardens.

Gardeners, commercial growers and consumers are not being encouraged to make the best use of what is available. The consequence of our disinterest and ignorance is that we end up with a limited choice and think of the potato as simply red or white.

For a variety to be traded as "seed" in the United Kingdom it must be included on the UK or EU national list. The breeders maintain the national list for those varieties covered by plant breeders' rights and the government for those produced more than 30 years ago but still wanted by growers.

The restrictions do not just affect old varieties. Many new varieties struggle to be included on the list because judgement has been made about yield at the expense of flavour. If consumer expectation is limited, we can hardly blame the breeders for growing varieties that contribute to so-called cheap food.

In the next few pages we will examine some of the popular and not so popular varieties. They have been assessed on experience and published data and judged on culinary and agronomic performance. Any recommendations are purely personal and biased - in the end, the celebration of the potato is its uniqueness and variety.

Varieties fall into three basic classes, depending on how long they take to grow. These are:

- First Earlies
- Second Earlies
- Maincrops

There are variations on all three. The classifications should be used as a guide, not as a rule. First earlies are usually fast-growing, lower-yielding new potatoes and maincrops the large winter supplies.

First Earlies

Accent (1989) - Of Dutch origin, early maturing and high yielding, especially if left in the ground to mature. Accent has a lemon-coloured flesh and close texture with a pleasing flavour. Has a bad reputation for blight and may suit lighter soils but watch for scab. Resistance to PCN (R).

Adora (1989) - Undistinguished Dutch variety with good early bulking capacity if you survive the blight susceptibility. It produces larger tubers than the average first early but the down side is the low numbers. Resistance to PCN (R).

Aminca (1977) - Another Dutch "also- ran" which has early bulking but blight, blackleg and scab susceptibility. Texture is close and waxy. PCN resistance.

Arran Comet (1956) - Outdated but a worthy performer. A pleasing fresh taste but delicate texture and declining quality when mature. The tubers are white fleshed and of an elongated shape

Arran Pilot (1930) - A classic. Once universally popular but now grown in small plots. Good taste and yields. Not the earliest of early varieties and does not like wet planting conditions.

Colleen (1993) - Interesting Irish offer with a pleasant taste and suits lighter soils. A good all-round performer but surprisingly for a new variety, no PCN resistance.

Colmo (1973) - The variety that knocked Arran Comet off its perch as the leading first early. This Dutch offering is similar to Colleen - slightly earlier and will put up with cool growing conditions. Flavour is undistinguished after the first pickings

Concorde (1988) - Dutch again but a worthy entry and widely grown. The long tubers and creamy flesh are often one of the first to appear. Taste is only fair, the texture wet and it has poor blight resistance.

Concurrent (1985) - So many Dutch varieties to choose from and often very similar. A good choice for those desperate to see the earliest new potatoes. Good resistance to PCN (R).

Duke of York (1891) - Still the benchmark for taste of all the new potato varieties. It has yellow skin and flesh and a reasonable yield. For best results grow on a light soil. The taste is aromatic and strong. The tubers disintegrate on cooking if the plant is left too long in the ground. An old variety prone to disease. Its sister variety, Red Duke of York, is visually stunning and eats well. Also a pink version.

Dundrod (1987) - I like this one. It's solid, durable and has good all round performance with taste a main feature. Better yield than Duke of York. Comparable to Accent including its poor tuber blight resistance. Resistance to PCN (R).

Dunluce (1976) - Very similar to Dundrod. Good one to choose if you want a slightly earlier potato with good culinary performance.

Epicure (1897) - Giant variety in stature. Loved and respected by Scottish growers in Ayrshire where it is still widely grown. Round tuber, not that early in maturing but with a mealy and distinctive taste. An old-fashioned potato very different to the waxy Duke of York or modern Dutch selections. Excellent recovery from frost damage.

Foremost (1954) - Good all-round potato but now dated. A sound choice if taste is high on your agenda as opposed to disease resistance which is limited. Again with these old types, don't plant too early; wait for the soil to warm up if you want the best from them.

First Earlies

Home Guard (1942) - Widely grown in Pembroke from the 1950's to 1980's Its culinary performance is poor, (after cooking it blackens). A major white-fleshed, round variety. Poor recovery from frost and needs plenty of water.

International Kidney (1879) - This is a second early variety better known as **Jersey Royal**. Grown on the rich, diverse and slightly saline soils of Jersey, this variety is shipped back to the UK and is one of the most sought-after potato varieties. International Kidney is difficult to grow and needs a very balanced soil. It needs to be harvested when young for best flavour which rapidly declines during the season.

Karlena (1993) - This German offering is a multi-purpose potato – good for roasting, chipping and frying in mid summer. It has good disease resistance and a mild taste. Resistant to PCN (R).

Maris Bard (1972) - Stylish and very popular British variety that keeps its bright white colour when cooked and allowed to cool. High yield but not the most flavoursome around. For the gardener, slugs will be a real challenge. Blight and blackleg could also be problems in wet seasons.

Pentland Javelin (1968) - British variety originating in Scotland. It is later than Maris Bard and other earlies. Good culinary quality. Its smooth, round shape and shallow eyes make it a good bet on the show bench.

Première (1979) - Interesting introduction from Holland. This variety has a firm waxy taste and good blight resistance. Slowly gaining in popularity. Not to be confused with Ulster Premier now off the national list.

Red Duke of York (1942) - Identical to Duke of York except that the skin is bright red, almost crimson. More vigour than Duke of York.

Rocket (1987) - As its name suggests, this British variety is fast growing and one of the first to produce a crop in the early summer. Good PCN resistance. Not my cup of tea as taste is lacking and it is prone to splitting.

Sharpe's Express (1901) - This old white-skinned, white-fleshed variety has a nice flavour but is hard to grow satisfyingly. Prone to blight and needs a rich soil with ample water. Collapses easily when cooked.

Ulster Chieftain (1938) - Ideal for growing in cloches or under polythene as the foliage produced is small. Tubers are white-fleshed. Sadly, its nice taste needs to be captured early. Don't leave in the ground as it may crack and hollow heart may set in.

Ulster Prince (1947) - The large, kidney-shaped tubers are worth the wait as this variety is not that early. If you are keen on growing Ulster varieties, the maturity sequence would be Sceptre, Chieftain, and then Prince.

Ulster Sceptre (1963) - One of the best post-war potatoes for yield and flavour. Yellow-fleshed with a close, almost waxy texture. Can be prone to blight.

Vanessa (1973) - Delicious red skinned variety which is prone to tuber blight.

Winston (1992) - A white-skinned, white-fleshed variety of good all-round quality developed by Jack Dunnet. Tubers form early and will hold in the ground if you want to keep them for later in the season as bakers. PCN Resistance (R).

Second Early and Maincrops

Ailsa (1989) - Competent, cream-skinned, white-fleshed variety which will perform all culinary functions well. Scottish in origin and would have gained greater popularity had it been equipped with PCN resistance.

Arran Banner (1927) - Famous variety from the great potato breeder, Donald Mackelvie. It fed Britain during the Second World War but not remembered with culinary affection. A bland variety if ever there was one.

Arran Victory (1918) - Purple skinned and with bright white flesh and delicious nutty taste, but mealy in texture. The foliage is extremely vigorous and late to mature. Ensure a well-structured soil if you want the best from Arran Victory.

Atlantic (1990) - A processing variety of considerable importance and good quality.

Ausonia (1981) - An improved version of Wilja, this second early has good all-round qualities including PCN Resistance (R).

Avalanche (1989) - Tremendous all-round qualities. Disappointing on light soils. Ensure a nice loam or a soil of body. Good culinary features. PCN (R) resistance.

Biamonda (1992) - Considered an improved Desiree but not for me. Lacks real flavour but its growing qualities are definitely better than Desiree, especially the PCN resistance to R.

Bintje (1910) - If we have our King Edward, the Dutch have their Bintje. Imported from Holland for years for the processing trade. Prone to blight.

British Queen (1894) - Moderate-yielding second early but fantastic flavour. A must for those who love potatoes and no wonder. It has kept its place in Ireland and parts of Scotland where they like a floury potato.

Cara (1976) - One of the most famous Irish varieties and deservedly as this late maincrop has excellent blight and PCN (R) resistance. It gives large sized tubers ideal for baking and on light to medium light soils, the flavour is good. Too much nitrogen and over watering will reduce this to quite a wet texture when cooked. Moderately prone to slug damage.

Carlingford (1982) - This second early is best grown as a new potato and will produce an abundance of small tubers with a good taste. Good for growing in tubs. Challenging Maris Peer as the new potato for midsummer. Shame it has no PCN resistance.

Catriona (1920) - A second early with real culinary class. Flavour, aroma and moderately floury texture make Catriona a real delight. Tubers can be large. Unfortunately susceptible to blight and other diseases.

Claret (1996) - Scottish answer to calls for an improved Desiree. Comparable to Biamonda but blight resistance is only moderate and no PCN resistance.

Desiree (1962) - Firm textured maincrop with a pinky red skin and distinctive taste. Excellent all-rounder in the kitchen and garden but misshapen when large. Despite a plethora of problems including susceptibility to virus, blight and PCN, Desiree has kept a dominant place in commercial crops, high yielding and accommodating most soils.

Dunbar Rover (1936) - A white-fleshed second early of close texture but good flavour. Not the yields of the modern second earlies.

Second Early and Maincrops

Dunbar Standard (1936) - Late maincrop with a highly vigorous foliage. The taste is distinctive and delicious. Needs plenty of water and will struggle on light soils.

Estima (1973) - The growers' choice. High yields, nice oval shape and suitable for all uses but excelling in none. Not grown organically due to its blight resistance, which is modest and no resistance to PCN.

Fianna (1987) - A Maris Piper imposter with PCN (R) resistance. Very high yielding and a slightly more floury texture. A nice variety to eat in early winter.

Golden Wonder (1906) - A famous old potato still loved for its very high floury texture. The pear-shaped, russet-skinned tubers are definitely distinctive but size and yield will disappoint. Its foliage is very vigorous and takes ages to reach maturity, but, for an old variety, it has some blight resistance.

Kerr's Pink (1917) - Still widely grown in Ireland where they seem to know a bit about good taste. This Scottish variety produces pink blushed tubers with a white flesh, floury texture and fine taste. Strong and vigorous foliage in a long growing season. Poor disease resistance.

Kestrel (1992) - Bred by Jack Dunnet of Caithness, this is to date the strongest variety in his portfolio. Delicious to eat and a good yield of attractive purple-blushed tubers with a cream flesh. Its medium dry-matter content makes the variety good for all main uses (boiling, chipping, roasting, mashing). Best used from August to January. Good PCN resistance to (R) and partial to (P). Its blight susceptibility is only marginally better than King Edward and that may prove decisive in its long-term organic future.

King Edward (1902) - The benchmark for culinary quality for 100 years, this red-blushed, creamy white-fleshed maincrop is still widely grown. A real challenge organically due to its susceptibility to most pests and diseases. Can produce a lot of tubers which require strong soils to build yield.

Kondor (1984) - Interesting Dutch offering which has a pleasing taste but not outstanding disease resistance. If you want a red skinned, yellow fleshed, waxy variety which is on the early side of maincrop then Kondor is the one for you.

Lady Rosetta (1992) - A crisping variety which, by definition, has a floury texture. Red skin, white flesh which has many positive features. Reasonable blight resistance and PCN (R).

Majestic (1911) - Once a universally popular maincrop with white flesh and skin. It has long dormancy so is best used in late winter. Large tubers and modest disease resistance. Not noted for its taste and the tubers discolour on medium to heavy soils.

Marfona (1975) - Introduced for the supermarkets with good claims about its taste. Its creamy coloured tubers are large and it tends to eat best early in the season. Slugs love this one and there is no PCN or assured blight resistance.

Maris Peer (1962) - Second early variety originally aimed for the canning market; now used as a mid summer potato. Superseded by Carlingford, the flesh is bright white and texture close. Good for boiling.

Maris Piper (1964) - Good all-rounder which dominates the commercial potato market and not the gardening landscape; for me, this says everything. On offer in every supermarket, it has to look nice and that is the challenge for Maris Piper growers. Prone to scab with poor blight resistance and a real slug catcher. However it does have resistance to PCN (R).

Second Early and Maincrops

Maxine (1993) - A Jack Dunnet variety with a red skin and wet to waxy texture. Best on dry soils. Good yield and PCN (R) resistance.

Mona Lisa (1982) - Its high yield of small, round, white-skinned and white-fleshed tubers helped get this variety established for the new potato trade. A second early.

Morene (1983) - Quietly gaining in reputation. A Dutch early maincrop with good all round resistance including PCN (R). Large clean tubers for baking.

Nadine (1987) - This variety is now number 4 in the UK acreage league table. It is resistant to PCN (R) and partially to (P) which makes it very alluring. However its taste is poor. Modern growing methods give this variety spectacular yields and slugs tend to avoid it.

Navan (1987) - Competent Northern Irish variety and a good alternative to Maris Piper with improved disease resistance, including PCN (R).

Nicola (1973) - Its long, yellow, waxy tubers are fine if indistinctive to eat. Will perform well in the kitchen and give good yields. A second early and very popular worldwide. Resistance to PCN (R). Good for boiling.

Pentland Crown (1959) - Outdated early maincrop from Scotland which produces large tubers with poor culinary quality. Its good disease resistance will ensure a crop.

Pentland Dell (1961) - Mostly used as a processing variety due to its high dry matter. The tubers are oval to kidney-shaped and large. Needs to be well sprouted and planted into warmish soils for best results. Now outdated.

Pentland Squire (1970) - Heavy-yielding variety with poor taste and not particularly good growing qualities. Suitable for all types of cooking but beware tuber discolouration.

Picasso (1992) - Dutch pink-eyed variety which is very high yielding and with PCN (R) resistance. Tuber-cracking and poor shape can sometimes occur. Moderate blight resistance.

Record (1932) - Old crisping variety now outdated but with a good flavour.

Red Cara (1976) - Identical to Cara but with red skin.

Red King Edward (1916) - Identical to King Edward but with 90% red skin. Very attractive for the show bench.

Remarka (1992) - Looks good on paper for the organic grower. Large yields of baking sized tubers. Pest and disease resistance are strong so what can go wrong? Not the most flavoursome maincrop variety. Resistance to PCN (R).

Romano (1978) - An early maincrop with vigorous growth, its red-skinned creamy flesh is very interesting. Its yield is fine, a bit below the modern standard and the culinary quality mixed. Poor on many conventional commercial systems but highly prized on allotments and under organic conditions. Romano is certainly worth a try. Slugs avoid it.

Russet Burbank (1878) - Fascinating variety. It has a russet skin, white flesh and tubular shape making it ideal for cutting into chips which are delicious. A special potato for special use. Once favoured by McDonald's for their chips but its susceptibility to blight may prove decisive. Still, it's been around for long enough. There are genetically modified stocks in the USA.

Second Early and Maincrops

Santé (1983) - The most popular organic variety due to its duel PCN (R) and partial (P) resistance. Good yields under most circumstances and suitable for most cooking purposes. To date, it is the pacesetter for organic farmers. Also popular conventionally.

Saturna (1962) - A variety almost exclusively for the crisp trade. Excellent for chips.

Saxon (1992) - Delicious white-skinned, white-fleshed UK variety that is slowly gaining popularity. Its mediocre blight resistance is holding it back. Plant in warm soils.

Stemster (1990) - Another red-skinned Jack Dunnet variety with high yields, low dry matter and PCN resistance (R). Culinary quality is fine for boiling. Slugs like this one but it does have good drought resistance.

Stroma (1989) - Red-skinned Jack Dunnet variety with good PCN Resistance (R) and partial (P). Again low dry matter so a good boiler but not so good for roasting or chipping.

Symfonia (1984) - Dutch introduction, modest yielding (for a modern variety) with high dry matter. Red skin, cream flesh, PCN (R) and good disease resistance.

Up To Date (1894) - An old variety with a waxy texture and pleasant taste. An interesting variety to grow, the foliage beautiful to look at, vigorous and very late.

Valor (1993) - Excellent late maincrop Jack Dunnet introduction which has massive yields and duel PCN (R) and (P) resistance. Tubers are bold and clean but once again low in dry matter. Back off on the watering and plant into light soils for best culinary results. Blight resistance is above average and this variety is too good to pass unnoticed.

Wilja (1967) - Dutch variety of very good culinary quality but outclassed by Nicola. Its lack of PCN resistance is a problem. Better than Estima on taste but agronomically slightly weaker.

Yukon Gold (1980) - The flavour and creamy buttery texture of this deep yellow-fleshed variety is superb but prone to blight and other diseases.

Salad Potatoes

Anya (1989) - An improved version of Pink Fir Apple? Judge for yourself.

Alex (1997) - Long tubers with blue splashed eyes. Its taste is lacking when compared to other salad types. Could do well on the show bench, but as yet, difficult to see where Alex fits in.

Belle De Fontenay (1885) - Classic French potato for use in salads. Its rich yellow flesh and waxy texture make it ideal. Great taste but susceptible to pests and diseases.

BF15 (1947) - This is a seedling from Belle De Fontenay. There is little to choose between the two but in my view BF15 has the edge in yield and flavour or is it just because I like the distinctive name?

Charlotte (1981) - I must be feeling charitable to include this as a salad potato but it is a good variety offering excellent creamy, waxy texture, flavour and reasonable disease resistance. Agronomically behind Nicola.

Linzer Delikatess (1976) - High-yielding, close-textured variety but flavour is not as good as other salad potatoes. Pear shaped tubers.

Pink Fir Apple (1850) - The UK salad potato retaining its dark flesh and waxy texture throughout the winter. Very long tubular pinkish tubers, very misshapen. Tubers form directly under foliage in clusters. Unfortunately the slugs still find them.

Ratte (1872) - The one to beat. It is long and tubular with a nutty yellow flesh and flavour we can only wish for in modern varieties. Prone to blight.

Roseval (1950) - Fine French salad potato with yellow flesh. It can be grown to a reasonable size and the tubers are versatile. Poor agronomically but well worth the effort.

Rare Varieties

There are many hundred of varieties which cannot be traded due to their non-national listing. Among them are some excellent eating types which deserve greater exposure to potato enthusiasts. Ones to look out for are:

Abundance - Early maincrop with good flavour.

Arran Rose - Kidney shaped and dark red skinned, this second early has a close texture and good taste.

Di Vernon - A first early with purple splashed skin and bright white flesh. Produces small foliage ideal for cloches.

Dr McIntosh - Second early with white skin and flesh. Heavy cropper and well-balanced flavour.

Eclipse - Second early with white flesh and a fine flavour.

Fortyfold - Purple skin and round shape with a striking yellow flesh which is buttery when cooked.

Highland Burgundy Red - Red-fleshed type of pleasant culinary quality. Medium sized tubers.

Mein's Early Round - Second early round tubers with striking red around the eyes. Ideal, floury autumn baker.

Myatts Ashleaf - Second early with white flesh and skin, a waxy texture and aromatic flavour.

Shetland Black - Part coloured flesh inside a bluish black skin. Dry and distinctive.

Sovereign - Very modern variety that does not give large yields but tastes delicious.

Violette - Stumpy, oval shape with blue flesh and a nice taste.

Recommended Potato List

BOIL NEW

- Duke of York
- Foremost
- Accent
- Dundrod
- Ulster Sceptre

BOIL

- Kestrel

MAINCROP

- Kondor
- Nicola
- Saxon
- Wilja

MASHING

- Desiree (creamy)
- Maris Piper (creamy)
- King Edward (creamy)
- Kerrs Pink (dry)
- Avalanche (creamy to dry)
- Lady Rosetta (dry)
- British Queen (dry)

ROASTING

- Maris Piper
- King Edward
- Romano (organic only)
- Desiree
- Lady Rosetta

BAKING

- Maris Piper
- King Edward
- Catriona
- Red Duke of York
- Yukon Gold

CHIP

- Russet Burbank
- Maris Piper
- Navan
- Pentland Dell
- Yukon Gold
- Ailsa

SALAD

- Ratte
- BF15
- Roseval
- Pink Fir Apple
- Belle De Fontenay

Recommended Potato List

BEST FOR ORGANIC GROWING

- Santé
- Romano
- Cara
- Symfonia
- Valor
- Première (as new potatoes)

BEST ALL ROUNDERS FOR COOKING

- Kestrel
- Desiree
- Maris Piper
- Wilja
- Saxon
- Avalanche

- Useful Reading and Contacts

- Conversion Tables

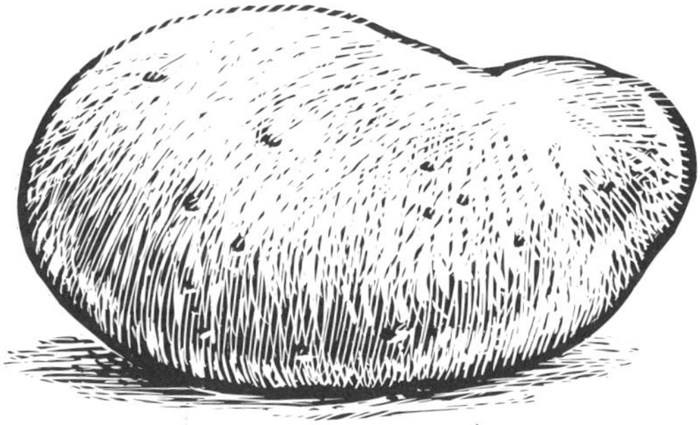

Useful Reading

The Story of the Potato - Alan Wilson

The Potato - Larry Zuckerman published by Macmillan

In Praise of the Potato - Lindsey Bareham published by Penguin

Alan Roman's Guide to Seed Potatoes

The Organic Directory - Clive Litchfield published by Green Books and The Soil Association

Useful Contacts

HDRA
Ryton Organic Gardens
Coventry CV8 3LG
Tel: 02476 303517
www.hdra.org.uk

There are an increasing number of potato days around the country. The original is held at Ryton Gardens during the first weekend in February every year and people come to it from far and wide – talks, displays, cookery demonstrations, the chance to buy from a variety of more than 100 seed potatoes and to meet up with other enthusiasts.

The Soil Association
Bristol House
40-56 Victoria Street, Bristol. BS1 6BY
Tel: 0117 929 0661
www.soilassociation.org

The British Potato Council
4300 Nash Court, John Smith Drive
Oxford Business Park South, Oxford OX4 2RT
Tel: 01865 714455
www.potato.org.uk

Our Favourite Organic Shops

Lots of shops now sell organic produce. As well as shopping at supermarkets, seek out local farm shops, independent retailers and farmers' markets for fresh, seasonal, local produce. Here are some of our favourites.

The Organic Farm Shop
Burford Road, Cirencester, Gloucestershire. GL7 5HF
Tel: 01225 640441
www.theorganicfarmshop.co.uk

Award-winning 100% organic farm shop with vegetables picked daily, meat from their own cattle, pigs and sheep and eggs from their own hens. Also bread, groceries, ice cream, wine etc. Trailer rides, café, cookery demonstrations and enthusiastic, knowledgeable staff.

The Walled Garden
6 Rose Terrace, Fort Royal Hill, Worcester. WR5 1BU
Tel: 01905 354629

Secluded herb garden near the city centre. Fresh and dried herbs, seeds and plants for sale. Limited opening so ring for details.

Ryton Organic Gardens
Coventry CV8 3LG
Tel: 02476 303517
Fax: 02476 639229
www.hdra.org.uk

HDRA's extensive shop selling food, wine, plants, books, gifts and gardening supplies. Also restaurant, gardens, vegetable box scheme, regular workshops, talks and demonstrations.

Our Favourite Organic Shops

The Village Bakery
Melmerby, Penrith, Cumbria. CA10 1HE
Tel: 01768 881515
www.village-bakery.com

Delicious organic bread and cakes made in wood-fired brick ovens. Lovely restaurant and shop selling books and some groceries. Hands-on bread making courses. Mail order available.

Audley End Kitchen Gardens
Saffron Walden, Essex. CB11 4JF
Tel/Fax: 01799 520 444

English Heritage and HDRA have restored this inspiring 10-acre Victorian walled kitchen garden in Essex. It is being managed organically and the fruit and vegetables are for sale in the shop.

Conversion Tables

There are lots of conversion tables around and these are the ones I use. Do remember to use either imperial or metric measurements.

30g	1oz
60g	2oz
85g	3oz
120g	4oz
150g	5oz
180g	6oz
200g	7oz
225g	8oz
250g	9oz
280g	10oz
320g	11oz
340g	12oz
375g	13oz
400g	14oz
425g	15oz
450g	16oz / 1lb
500g	1lb 2oz
675g	$1\frac{1}{2}$lb
900g	2lb
1kg	$2\frac{1}{4}$lb
$1\frac{1}{2}$kg	3lb 6oz

Conversion Tables

30ml	1 fl oz	2 tbsp
60ml	2 fl oz	4 tbsp
90ml	3 fl oz	6 tbsp
120ml	4 fl oz	
150ml	5 fl oz	$\frac{1}{4}$ pint
180ml	6 fl oz	
210ml	7 fl oz	
240ml	8 fl oz	
270ml	9 fl oz	
300ml	10 fl oz	$\frac{1}{2}$ pint
330ml	11 fl oz	
360ml	12 fl oz	
390ml	13 fl oz	
420ml	14 fl oz	
450ml	15 fl oz	$\frac{3}{4}$ pint
480ml	16 fl oz	
510ml	17 fl oz	
540ml	18 fl oz	
570ml	19 fl oz	
600ml	20 fl oz	1 pint
750ml	$1\frac{1}{4}$ pints	
900ml	$1\frac{1}{2}$ pints	
1 litre	$1\frac{3}{4}$ pints	
1.2 litres	2 pints	

- Index

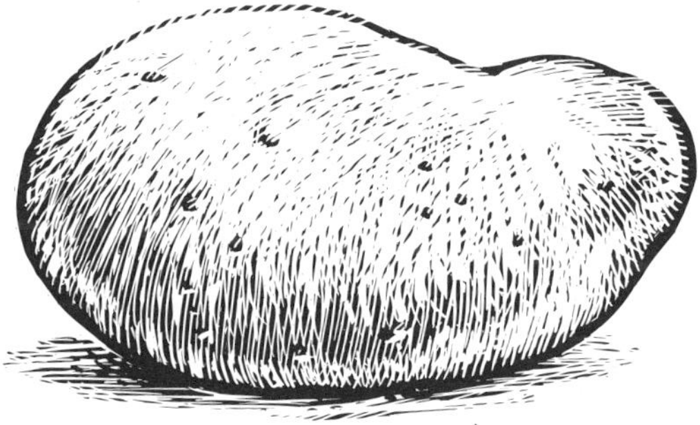

Potato Varieties – 134-149

2004 FIRST EARLY / PENTLAND JAVELIN
VERY GOOD CROP NO TASTE

MAINCROP / CARA / BAKING

MAINCROP / SANTE ORGANIC "